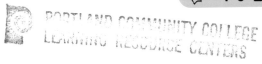

THINK About

Prisons and the Criminal Justice System

The THINK Series Editors: William N. Thorndike, Jr.
                         Ramsey R. Walker

Executive Editor: Doug Hardy
Researcher: Martha T. Griffith

Jacket Designer: Georg Brewer
Text Designer: Joyce C. Weston
Copyeditor: Victoria Haire
Photo Researcher: Diane Hamilton
Text Illustrator: Peter Zale
Research Assistant: Caitlin Dixon

The THINK Series

THINK About

Prisons and the Criminal Justice System

Lois Smith Owens, M.S.W., and Vivian Verdell Gordon, Ph.D.

Walker and Company
New York

First published in the United States of America in 1992 by Walker Publishing Company, Inc.

Published simultaneously in Canada by Thomas Allen & Son Canada, Limited, Markham, Ontario

Library of Congress Cataloging-in-Publication Data
Owens, Lois Smith.
    Think about prisons and the criminal justice system / Lois Smith Owens and Vivian Verdell Gordon.
        p.   cm.—(The Think series)
    Includes bibliographical references and index.
    Summary: Discusses various aspects of prison and the criminal justice system, how they evolved, whether they are effective, and what may lie in the future.
    ISBN 0-8027-8121-7. —ISBN 0-8027-7370-2 (pbk.)
    1. Criminal justice, Administration of—United States—Juvenile literature.   2. Prisons—United States—Juvenile literature.   [1. Prisons.   2. Criminal justice, Administration of.]   I. Gordon, Vivian Verdell.   II. Title.   III. Series.
HV9950.O84   1992
364.973—dc20   91-2860
                                                                CIP
                                                                AC

Printed in the United States of America

10 9 8 7 6 5 4 3 2 1

To our fathers and our sons

CONTENTS

ACKNOWLEDGMENTS

We wish to thank our families, who are always there for us. Special thanks go to John P. Whiting and Lester J. Brown, who encouraged and supported us in this work. They are also always there for us.

A special thank you is also extended to Useni Perkins, who guided much of our thinking about the consequences to young people involved in criminal behavior, and Haki R. Madhubuti, who has influenced our thinking about some of the particular conditions that confront Black men.

We gratefully acknowledge the patience and guidance of the press editor at Walker, Doug Hardy. The excellent manuscript preparation was the work of our editorial typist, Fran Lassiter. We wish to thank Linda Thurston, who recommended us to Doug.

We continue to learn from our conversations with men and women who are prisoners. They have helped us better understand some of the family and community support that they need in order to return as positive and productive participants in society. We wish to encourage them to take full advantage of all existing programs that could help them become better prepared for their futures.

INTRODUCTION

Why do societies have laws?
What is the difference between a rule and a law?
When did laws begin?
How did one young man get involved in crime?

This book will help you think about prisons, crime and its consequences, and the criminal justice system. The criminal justice system is concerned with safety, individual rights, and the rules by which people enforce the laws of their society.

As you follow the story of one young man in prison, you will learn about crime and its consequences as well as the kinds of institutions that have been established for those who violate the law. You will also learn about the different kinds of institutions that isolate, restrict, punish, and promote rehabilitation for criminals.

In television and movies, especially old movies, the life of a criminal is exciting and fun. Heroic criminals are shown outwitting the police and others. Many young people know only the movie version of prisons. Through this book, we hope that some of those wrong images will be corrected. Clearly, we want you to understand that there is nothing exciting and adventurous about being in a prison or jail. Nor is there any excitement in any of the other places to which people are sent to pay their debt to society.

Very little attention is usually given to the programs within prisons and other institutions of the criminal justice system that help people understand what they have done wrong against society. These programs are designed to help ex-offenders prepare themselves for a positive and productive life upon release. Using the information available, we will tell you what can and should be done to help ex-offenders.

As you read, we hope that you will ask yourself questions such as:

- What is a crime?
- Why do people commit crime?
- When is a person a criminal?
- How are laws enforced?
- How does the justice system work?
- What are the forms of imprisonment, and how are they different?
- What are some of the problems within the present system, and what new programs are helping to resolve them?
- What about the family and friends of people who are imprisoned?

We hope that after you read this book, you will better understand prisons and the justice system. Perhaps you'll want to learn more about a career in criminal justice. Or you may wish to team up with your teacher or family and meet and talk to people who are lawyers, judges, social workers, juvenile probation officers, parole officers, police officers, counselors, criminologists, psychologists, sociologists, or religious leaders—all of whom work in some very important part of the justice system.

CEDRICK'S STORY

It is 7:00 A.M., and Cedrick's mother has arrived early at the bus stop. The shuttle bus, which takes people for visits with their family or friends who are in prison, arrives about 7:30. Mrs. Blount seats herself in the front of the bus, so she can have a clear view of the country-side during the two-hour trip. The state prison is more than 100 miles away.

On the way to the prison, the bus travels through many small towns. From the bus window, Mrs. Blount is able to see homes and shopping centers; city parks and high schools with their football fields; apartment buildings and office buildings; churches, synagogues, and mosques; and people driving or waiting to ride the bus to their jobs in shops and factories. Seeing all this makes Mrs. Blount think about the different people she knows, her neighbors, friends, and the people at her job. She realizes that she knows people who are of many different cultures. Mrs. Blount wonders how neighborhoods, towns, and cities are formed. What makes a society?

In one small town, Mrs. Blount looks across the street to the park where she sees mothers and fathers walking or watching children at play. She remembers how much fun it was when she would take Cedrick, his brother, and sister to the park. Now, it will be a long time before Cedrick will be free to travel and enjoy the outdoors. Mrs. Blount begins to ask herself many questions about why Cedrick, who is now eighteen, ended up in prison.

Cedrick's father worked on weekends, as well as during the week, because only with two jobs could he support his family. Most of the time, Cedrick and his brother and sister went to the park and other places with his mother or with older friends who had promised to look after them. But sometimes, when both his mother and his father had been at work, or when his mother had been busy at home with the care of his brother and sister, Cedrick would go to the park alone.

On his own, Cedrick made friends with children his parents did not like. His parents told Cedrick that some of the boys and one of the girls he knew had "been in trouble," but Cedrick did not pay much attention. He thought that no one could make him do anything he did not want to do. Besides, he wanted friends, and he was flattered that the older guys he had met were allowing him to be part of their group. Often, they paid him to run errands to the cleaners and to do other small jobs for them. Cedrick thought that his parents just did not understand how important it was to belong.

One time, someone in the group told him to take a bike that was leaning against the playground wall. The others thought it would be a good joke, since they did not like the boy who owned the bike anyway. That was the first time that Cedrick had stolen anything.

Cedrick was not caught that time, and he began to steal more things. His new friends approved. Neither Cedrick, with his part-time job, nor his parents could afford such things. When he took expensive items, Cedrick thought to himself that the person who owned them could just buy others. These thoughts helped him justify his stealing.

One day, Cedrick and his friends stole a car. Thinking that the owner might return to the car before they could get away, one member of the group had taken a gun with him. The stolen car was very expensive, and Cedrick and his friends thought they'd get a lot of money by selling it to illegal dealers in auto parts. They were caught by the police, who learned that they had stolen other things and then sold them.

Mrs. Blount and her husband love their children and had taught Cedrick about honesty. They believed him when he said that he had bought the things he stole with money from his part-time job. He could have purchased some of the things at reasonable prices in any one of a number of discount stores in the area. Whenever his father warned Cedrick about people who "would get him into trouble," Cedrick denied that he had such friends. He had in fact considered leaving the group, but it gave him praise, support, status, and made him a leader.

It is important to remember that many young people grow up today in situations where there is limited recreation; where there are groups of gangs that encourage illegal behavior; and where there is little opportunity to earn money to buy the things that are advertised so widely. But even under these conditions, most young people do not commit crimes.

WHY WE HAVE LAWS

What is law, and why are laws necessary? To answer this question, we should begin by talking about communities. Think about the different towns and cities through which Mrs. Blount's bus passed on the way to the prison. Communities such as these are formed when groups of people voluntarily come together in an exchange of work and reward. We usually think that the reward for work is money, but money is only the means by which work can be converted into goods (such as food and houses) or services (such as police work and teaching).

When we use the term *society*, we are speaking about the many small communities that, as they grow in size and number, we call a state and, on a large scale, a nation. Each of us is a member of a local community, a citizen of a state, and a citizen of the nation (the larger community or society). Each community teaches its basic values, norms (primary beliefs about right and wrong), and expected behaviors in a process called *socialization*. Communities reward behavior that meets their expectations, and punish behavior that does not. The process happens primarily at home, where young children are encouraged and rewarded when they behave in keeping with the expectations of their communities. They are discouraged when they behave otherwise.

In a free and democratic society, all citizens participate in the formulation of rules and regulations. Some of the rules are more important than others, and they become laws. Since families cannot usually provide all the teaching and reward that an individual needs, institutions such as schools, churches, and health centers help through educational support.

Communities operate by many informal rules, which are not laws, but which are followed by common practice, belief, and traditions. If these rules are broken, a person might not be liked, but the person is *not* a criminal.

An individual is a criminal only when that person is found to be guilty of violating one of the laws of the community. Laws reflect the will of the communities at the local, state, and national levels, and violations of those laws result in punishment by the legal and criminal justice system.

LOCAL, STATE, AND FEDERAL LAWS

Since people must be able to live and work together, while at the same time maintaining their differences, they must have some process for making and enforcing their laws. Laws are designed to protect individual and group rights, to protect the innocent and those who might be exploited, and to preserve the communities' norms.

In a democracy, people elect representatives for whom the process of law is a primary duty. In cities and towns, the governing board is often a town or city council. At the state level, there are state representatives and state senators, and at the national level, there are the elected members of the House of Representatives and the Senate.

Society makes laws as a means of regulating social control, although social control also depends on many other factors. In some societies the people form tribal councils for this purpose; in other societies the people must abide by the decisions of rulers such as kings and queens. In still other societies citizens are subject to rules and laws forced upon them by invading armies or conquerors. In the United States the system of law is administered through the judicial system, which we will discuss later.

How many different societies do you know about? Do you know how they established rules and regulations? Do you know about the nations of the Native Americans? Do you know the systems of justice established over 3,000 years ago in ancient African civilizations? Do you know about the systems of justice of early China, the Middle East, and Europe? Many of these systems influenced ours.

A MOTHER'S VISIT

The bus has arrived at the prison, and the guard has released the gate lock so that the bus can enter the prison grounds. Now Mrs. Blount and the others will finally be able to have a short visit with family and friends; they walk to the visitor's entrance. Mrs. Blount sighs when she thinks about how young her son is and how far away he is from his family. She wonders what went wrong and why Cedrick committed the crimes that resulted in his imprisonment.

Mrs. Blount and the others wait in line at the prison office. They are required to sign in, giving their name, address, the time of day, and the name of the prisoner they are visiting. They are also subject to a personal inspection. The man who is in line in front of Mrs. Blount is told at the counter that he cannot take his cassette recorder into the visitor's room because such items are not allowed. When it is Mrs. Blount's turn, her purse is emptied and all the contents are examined. She is allowed to take her wallet and her glasses case with her into the visitor's room. But she must remove her house keys and any other metal objects from her purse and pockets, so that she can pass through the metal detector. No item that can be used as a weapon is allowed in the visitor's room. Mrs. Blount's keys—as well as any other items that might be confiscated, such as a fingernail file or a metal comb—will be returned to her after the visit. When she has completed this routine, called the *intake process*, she gets her left hand stamped so that she can be identified as a visitor. Finally, the guards escort Mrs. Blount and the others into the visiting area.

When Cedrick enters the room, he sees the face of a very sad mother who loves him and who will do all she can to sustain him while he pays his debt to the community—that is, while he "serves time" in the prison. Cedrick is very happy when his mother holds his hand

and tells him how much she loves him and how she and his family anxiously await his return. Since Cedrick is in a minimum-security section of the prison, his mother does not have to visit with him through a glass partition while speaking over a telephone. The ability to enjoy a more personal visit is one of the privileges of Cedrick's minimum-security status.

It is very difficult for families to make the long journey to visit prisons. Prisons are not usually located on train or bus routes, and many families do not own cars. Cedrick is very lucky that his mother and his father can take turns visiting him each month. When there are special events, his parents bring his young brother and sister (they do not come often, because it is difficult for the young children to make the long trip and sad for them to see their brother in prison). Cedrick is fortunate to have the continued love, concern, and support of his family. As we will discuss at the conclusion of the book, such family support will be important when Cedrick finishes his sentence and returns to his community.

The original purpose of prisons in America was not only to punish people but also to help them become better persons. It was thought that if a person was sentenced to prison, he or she would feel punished enough to want to stop committing crimes. This view about the purpose of prisons is usually called a *just deserts model*. (You have probably heard the saying "He got his just deserts"—or what he deserved.) It is also referred to as *deterrence and retribution*.

REVIEW QUESTIONS

1. Can a community function without laws?
2. What are some things that you think Cedrick's par-

ents might have done when he began to be friends with a group that might get him into trouble?

3. Since Cedrick had been taught better, why do you think he continued to commit crimes?

4. How would you explain to his younger sister and brother why Cedrick was in prison?

5. What might Cedrick have done to prevent his going to prison?

6. Why do you suppose that prisons and other institutions for imprisonment are located far away from major cities and towns?

7. Can you tell about some of the systems of justice of other societies?

8. If you and the families on your block were to form an independent town, what are some of the rules and regulations you think you would need to make?

9. Give an example of a rule in your community that is usually followed, but which is not a law.

1 | When People Commit Crime

WHY DO PEOPLE COMMIT CRIME?

Although we know why some people commit crimes, no one knows exactly why different people commit the many different kinds of crime.

People commit crime for a variety of reasons:

- because they want things they cannot afford or for which they do not have the money.
- because they think that it is fun to hurt others and to profit from their victims
- because it makes them feel important—it makes them a hero within their group by proving they are "tough" or a "big timer"
- because they think it is the only way out of a difficult situation
- because they have not been taught the norms—that is, the rules and expected behavior—of their communities
- because they are around people who have committed crimes and they have not learned any other forms of behavior
- because they are addicted to substances—drugs—that affect their body chemistry, resulting in aggressive and violent behavior

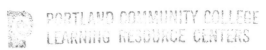

- because they are addicted to drugs that are expensive, and their addiction makes them willing to do anything to get a continuing supply of these drugs
- because they are not aware of the law they have violated.

Regardless of the reason, when the law is violated, a crime has been committed. When a person has been found guilty of violating the law, that person is guilty of a crime. *It is wrong to commit a crime. It is wrong because it is against the law!* Remember, when we began, we talked about communities and societies and the reasons people come together to live cooperatively. We pointed to the need for rules and regulations—for laws that must be observed by all to promote and maintain an orderly process, to secure justice, and for the protection of the innocent.

ARE ALL LAWS JUST?

Some people believe that certain laws are unjust, and that they are victims of discrimination, or unequal justice. These persons might knowingly break a law to force a decision about whether or not that law is just or to force the public to pay attention to what they maintain is an injustice. American history is full of examples of such actions. During the American Revolution, for example, participants in the Boston Tea Party violated the law to protest what they thought was an unjust tax.

During the civil rights movement of the 1950s and 1960s, many people of all races and religious backgrounds violated racist state laws. These actions, called *civil disobedience*, were taken in the name of morality. When protesters broke laws they felt were wrong, they were fully aware of the fact that they could be arrested and put in jail, and many hundreds of them were in fact arrested and jailed. They were willing to face the consequences of their actions because they believed the judicial system would recognize the unjust nature of the laws and would then dismiss the legal charges against them.

Protest actions continue to this day. For example, advocates for the disabled have been arrested for blocking entrances of buildings and those who support the homeless have intentionally violated anti-loitering laws, to call attention to their cause. Although many would say that these crimes are not serious, the violators still know they can be arrested and jailed and brought before the court for judgment. The point is that they commit crimes in order to change the law, not for personal or material gain.

WHAT IS A CRIME, AND WHO IS A CRIMINAL?

A crime is a wrong that one or more persons commits against others by violating the laws of the society. It may be an action that does direct harm to others, such as stealing. It may be an action that puts others in danger or infringes upon their rights (for example, driving when under the influence of alcohol). Although crimes have both a moral and a legal meaning, by definition, *a crime is a particular wrong that is judged to violate the law.* As a result of a crime, harm is done to a person or to the society, and *restitution*—that is, payment for damages—must be made. In another section, we will talk about the various forms of penalty.

There are differing degrees of legal violations, from very minor to very serious. All violations of laws result in *sanction*, or punishment, by citizens through their legal systems. The more serious violations receive more serious sanction.

History shows that people of all different times and cultures have adopted systems of laws and systems to punish those who violate their laws. All laws have their origins in the belief systems of the people of that society. The importance of individual laws to a culture is reflected in the seriousness of the punishment given to violators of the laws.

In a free and democratic society, the laws reflect the will of the majority and are enacted through a democratic process that allows for representation of the cultural diversity. It is not always easy for those who are elected or appointed to develop fair and just legislation. Care must always be taken to ensure that the laws do not deny citizens their human rights or their rights to have different beliefs as long as they do not threaten the safety and security of others. In the United States, the Constitution provides the guide for the protection of the rights of individual citizens. However, having a differing opinion or belief does not give a person the right to victimize another, that is, take advantage through power, threat, or force.

We must be careful not to conclude that a person is a criminal when that person is *thought* to have done something wrong. An individual is not a criminal until it has been *proven* that the person did commit the crime. In America, a person is innocent until proven guilty. This is why the justice system must be fair and why good legal representation must be avail-

A chief feature of prisons has always been regimentation of daily life. (Clinton prison, 1912, Dannemore, New York) (Courtesy of The Library of Congress)

able to all citizens regardless of their beliefs, their race, their age, or whether they are rich or poor.

We began this book by telling you about Cedrick, a young man who is now in prison because he committed a crime. Perhaps Cedrick needed to feel important, or maybe he was encouraged to break the law by friends. Perhaps Cedrick's part-time job did not pay him enough money to buy some of the things he wanted; perhaps, in spite of the fact that he was taught his community's beliefs about right and wrong, Cedrick had not internalized those values and was able to put them aside when the opportunity presented itself. No one can list all the various personal needs and attitudes that together resulted in his decision to break the law. There is no hard-and-fast answer to explain why an individual commits crime.

WHITE-COLLAR CRIME

When most people think of crime, they imagine violent crimes such as murder, robbery, and assault. Television and movies depict this sort of crime most often. When we talk about crime, it is easy to imagine these acts of violence.

Another group of crimes, called *white-collar crime*, is thought about less often. Many people do not consider these violations of the law to be "real" or "major" crimes because they do not think that these crimes have victims. In fact, there are victims in white-collar crime—but the offender does not usually have direct contact with them. White-collar crime includes embezzlement (stealing money entrusted to you, as in a bank), fraud (misleading people to get their money or property), and violation of business laws for personal gain. A recent example of white-collar crime was the "insider trading" by which certain businesspeople used confidential information for unfair gain in the stock market.

White-collar crimes are more likely (but not always) to be committed by people who have unusual skills (most often skills that require high levels of education or training). Because these crimes often involve large sums of money and at the same time do not result in immediate visible suffering by the victims (hundreds of people), it is difficult for people to remember that what has been done is against the law and is therefore a crime. Nevertheless, when a person embezzles a million dollars from his or her workplace, that person is a criminal. The Federal Bureau of Investigation (FBI) has reported that white-collar crime in the United States totals approximately $100 billion a year.

Amazingly, and many would say unfairly, when such persons are caught, they are seldom brought before the criminal courts. For this reason, their violations of the law are not usually considered to be a crime—certainly not a serious crime. In fact, the FBI includes embezzlement under its list of Part II offenses; that is, it is not classified as a serious crime. Since the most immediate victim of white-collar crime is usually the workplace of the criminal, the most serious cases are often resolved by administrative agencies or through the informal structures of very specialized law firms. Some examples of white-collar crime are the following:

The Cost of White-Collar Crime (in Billions of Dollars)*

Bankruptcy fraud	$ 0.21
Bribery, kickbacks, and payoffs	7.74
Computer-related crime	0.26
Consumer fraud, illegal competition, deceptive practices	54.18
Credit-card and check fraud	2.84
Embezzlement and pilferage	18.06
Insurance fraud	5.16
Receipt of stolen property	9.03
Securities thefts and frauds	10.32
Total (billions)	$107.80

As you can see from this table, it is clearly wrong to think that white-collar crime is a victimless crime. To be a victim does not always require physical and immediate personal abuse.

*Source: Chamber of Commerce of the United States, *A Handbook on White-Collar Crime*, 1974 (figures adjusted for inflation and population growth through 1991; subtotals do not sum to totals due to rounding).

RACE, GENDER, AND SOCIAL CLASS

When a person is alleged to have committed a crime, he or she is arrested and brought before the courts for trial and judgment. When we look at the statistics that report who is arrested as well as who is imprisoned, we find that a larger percentage of persons who are arrested and in judicial custody are nonwhite and poor. Given these data, it is easy to conclude that those persons are more criminal in their behavior than are other persons, but that is not necessarily true.

Historians, sociologists, criminologists, and other persons who specialize in the study of minority groups can document that many people are victimized because of prejudice based on race, religion, gender, and social class. This prejudice has often resulted in discrimination against certain individuals and/or groups. *Prejudice* is a preconceived attitude or belief, usually negative, about persons or groups; this attitude and belief remains fixed even in the face of information that proves it to be false. When persons act on their prejudice, that is called *discrimination* (see the Think series book *Racism*).

Discrimination can be based on a person's or a group's ethnicity, religion, race, or gender. Discrimination results in unfair treatment for such persons. When society discriminates, it is called *institutionalized racism*. That is, the structure and the administration of the social institutions (schools, executive and judicial branches of government) have been influenced by and reflect the prejudices that have existed over many years. *Racism* results from prejudice based on ethnicity, culture, race, and so on. *Sexism* results from prejudice based on male or female gender or on a person's choice of sexual partner. *Classism* results from prejudice based on social class, such as whether the person is rich or poor.

We cannot discuss the criminal justice system as a social institution without paying attention to problems or flaws that result from racism, sexism, and classism. The system has some of the same problems that exist within the society at large. As noted, nonwhite people and poor people are arrested more often than other persons. When arrested, they are kept in jails while awaiting trial, often because they do not have the money for bail or for the best legal representation.

Many of the poor people who are arrested do not have family, friends, and neighbors in high places who can immediately call the police precinct to speak on their behalf. Most often, they have no one to quickly come to their assistance. Even if these people are not found guilty of a crime, the arrest records of the police department will still report that an arrest was made.

In addition, since poor people rarely have the money to pay for bail or to hire an attorney to give them quick personal service, many are jailed on "suspicion" and must wait until a court-appointed attorney can meet with them and help them establish their innocence. Sometimes, those persons do not even have the opportunity to talk to the court-appointed attorney until the time they appear before a judge, and thus very little time has been given to preparing their defense.

Court-appointed attorneys tend to be overworked, with heavy caseloads of persons who need their

At the turn of the century, a disproportionate number of prisoners were African-American. This is still true. (Southern chain gang, ca. 1900) (Courtesy of The Library of Congress)

services. Some organizations that have given special attention to the legal needs of the poor have reported that, very frequently, court-appointed attorneys are new to the profession and thus lack experience. This combination—very large caseloads, limited time for preparation, and inexperienced attorneys—often results in inadequate representation for the poor.

To these negative factors, we must add the tendency to wrongly presume that the poor are criminals. There appears to be a very strong correlation between income and education, and the limited education of very poor persons hurts their ability to communicate properly with those in authority or even to clearly understand the legal process, which increases the likelihood for them to be in prison.

Although many court-appointed lawyers are hardworking and dedicated advocates, others do not always give their best efforts. The reason is simple: they receive very low pay for their work compared with those lawyers in private practice; so sometimes they resent having to defend poor people.

It is difficult to determine when someone is arrested (and then found guilty in a court of law) solely on the basis of his or her personal appearance or limited communication skills. There are an increasing number of community-based legal-aid organizations and advocate groups that work hard to call attention to factors that influence the arrest rates of very low-income or poor people. But their task is not easy. Many people become upset and even outraged when any question is raised about flaws in the judicial process.

An equally difficult topic to discuss is racism. Many studies have reported that nonwhite persons are arrested more often than whites because they are victims of prejudice and discrimination by law enforcement officers, or because they live in neighborhoods where there are more frequent police patrols.

We also know that criminal statistics (the number of arrests recorded and reported) vary from police district to police district, because there is no uniform means for the collection of such information. Although the information is published in so-called uniform crime reports, social scientists tell us that many factors—including race, status (rich or poor), and even personal appearance or place of residence— appear to have some impact on whether a given individual is more likely to be arrested and brought before the criminal court.

Just as racism results from preconceived attitudes about people of particular races, sexism results from such attitudes about a given gender. Many people have prejudicial attitudes about what is appropriate behavior for women as compared with men. For people who are sexist (they can be male or female), any attitude or behavior that differs from what has been very rigidly defined as appropriate for women is suspect. Some studies have reported that women who are not "where women should be" are suspect in this way. For example, it has been said that boys who might gather on the corner to talk and enjoy the company of a group are not viewed with as much displeasure as girls who do the same. Other studies have reported that the attitude about girls who run away from home differs from that about boys who do the same, because of the stereotype that says boys are expected to have adventures.

Currently, about 43,845 women are imprisoned in

state and federal correctional institutions. Although we do not know all the reasons why imprisonment among women is increasing, we do know that a greater number of girls and women are becoming involved in more serious crimes than in the past. We do know that many girls and women are committing serious and violent crimes that are associated with or related to substance abuse.

There are studies that tell us something about women in prison. It is reported that prison life for women is much like that for men, with some exceptions. One such exception is that imprisoned women are likely to be housed together in the same facility regardless of the differing degrees of seriousness of their crimes. Also, while there is often not enough work for all the men who are imprisoned, there is even less work available for the women. The work that is available is seldom meaningful or educational. It is most often cleaning, cooking, and sometimes sewing—duties that have traditionally been considered to be women's work.

Prison programs that teach technical skills required for certain types of employment are not as readily available for women as for men, although a few facilities do offer them. You may know, of course, that a number of people believe an education in technology, science, and math is inappropriate for girls and women. Fortunately, such attitudes are changing and must continue to change. In the future, more and more jobs will require technical skills. Women in prisons must be as adequately prepared for meaningful and rewarding employment when they return to their communities.

Because prisons were initially designed for men,

limited attention has been given to the needs of women who are imprisoned. They are often bored, receive fewer and more limited opportunities for physical fitness, and are restricted in occupational-training choices.

Although parenting is equally important for men and women, by tradition the care of young children has been primarily a female responsibility. Women in prison are especially limited in their roles as parents because they are generally unable to have contact with their children on a regular basis. Since there is no separation of women offenders into minimum-, medium-, or maximum-security prisons, and since their numbers are fewer, resulting in fewer facilities, women can be imprisoned as much as 1,000 miles from their home communities.

Although male facilities are usually located some distance away from major cities and towns, these distances are often not as far away as those for many women's prisons. You can readily understand how much more difficult it is for women who wish to have regular visits from their families, and especially their young children. The situation is equally stressful for families who wish to maintain contact in order to support the women who are their mothers, sisters, wives, and girlfriends.

It also appears that very limited attention has been given to the particular health needs of women in prison. Although many facilities provide prenatal care and for childbirth, and some facilities now allow mothers to keep their babies with them for extended periods, when the mother is imprisoned her children at home are most likely to be placed in foster homes or with relatives.

Sometimes the foster parents make no effort to sustain the child-mother relationship. One reason may be the cost and time involved; or they may feel that the children should not be exposed to prisons and jails.

REVIEW QUESTIONS

1. What is a crime?
2. What do we mean when we say that a person is innocent until proven guilty, and why is this especially important in a free and democratic society?
3. Can you think of reasons that a person might commit a crime or crimes, other than those we have suggested?
4. What do you think about the morality of civil disobedience? What do you know about the Boston Tea Party, the civil rights movement, and the current movements that violate laws in protest?
5. What do we mean by the term *white-collar crime?* Who are its victims? What are some things that you think can be done about white-collar crime?
6. Do you think that people who commit "big business crimes" should be prosecuted in criminal court like a person who stole $1,000 or a car?
7. Why do you think that such limited attention has been given to issues related to women in prison?
8. Are there ways by which more equitable representation can be made available to the poor who are accused of crimes?
9. What are some things that you think can be done

to change the prejudices that are based on the current reporting of arrest rates for nonwhite persons?

10. What factors might contribute to a higher arrest and incarceration rate among nonwhite and poor people?

2 History and Debate: Law Enforcement and the Courts

How have police changed over the years?
What are the two main court systems?
What does a prosecutor do?
What does a judge do?
What is the difference between a defense attorney and a public defender?

THE HISTORY OF POLICING

Some form of policing has taken place in every society. In some less complex communities of the past, the means for controlling those who harmed others were simple and direct. People who did not obey the rules of the community or caused harm to someone would be targets of vengeance, with the approval of the community.

In other less complex societies, people accused of crimes were brought before a group of peers where they faced charges and had an opportunity to defend themselves. If they were found guilty, they received particular forms of punishment. In other words, throughout history there have been systems of law, justice, and retribution in many societies and cultures, not just our own.

The protection of the community has been a requirement of all societies. Protection has been required from both without and within—to defend from hostile outsiders and to defend from those who would violate the rules of the community. Years ago in England, families were organized into what was called the *frankpledge system*. First, the families were grouped into ten family organizations, called *tithings*, and then regrouped into hundreds, in order to protect themselves. Under that system, all members of the frankpledge were responsible to one another and would be fined if they failed to arrest one who broke the law.

As societies became larger and more complex, different forms of control were developed. In England at the beginning of the twelfth century, sheriffs enforced the law. The term *sheriff* was derived from the word *shire*, which was originally used to define the boundaries of land, much like the way we define a county. The sheriff was appointed by the king and had the responsibility for the safety of the entire county. Later, the sheriff structure was extended, and he was assisted by constables whom he appointed. The constable was assigned the task of maintaining order and the care of all community weaponry. A watch system, much like our neighborhood watch system, was devised to protect property as well as to maintain law and order. While these men carried weapons, they did not wear uniforms (perhaps setting the trend for the first undercover policemen). In the beginning, they worked at night; later, it became necessary for a day shift to be added.

As societies became even more complex, problems began to surface and the rate of crime began to increase. Public drinking, violent and inappropriate behavior, and theft increased, and this led to the need for a more formalized approach to policing.

The English began very early to try different forms of policing. The Bow Street Runners was a group whose job was to investigate crimes and arrest suspects as well as to maintain safety. They were paid a commission based on those cases with which they were successful. In the city of London, concern for safety was directed toward improving protection, and in 1829 the Metropolitan Police of London was established. Because they were founded by Sir Robert Peel, they were first known as *peelers;* another name for them was *bobbies,* which is still used today. They were assigned to territories, and they wore uniforms. Most important, they were required to meet certain standards in order to become police officers.

The United States patterned its policing on the English model. In very early days, sheriffs were in charge of counties and constables were in charge of towns. Both were appointed by the governors at first and later elected through an electoral process. Here, as in England, sheriffs were paid by the fee system. Marshals enforced the laws in the cities, where they were assisted by constables, watchmen, city council members, and police justices. Each community was responsible for taking care of its own.

In the Southern states prior to the Civil War, there were *slave patrols* with the primary responsibility of recapturing escaped slaves. In the West, *vigilantes* or

volunteer police, prevented crimes such as cattle rustling. As the nation developed and as cities grew, these practices were not sufficient to maintain law and order. New ways to police were needed. The city of Boston developed its police department in 1838, New York in 1845, and Philadelphia in 1850. Those departments were established in the aftermath of urban riots and violence. Police jobs were highly desirable because they paid a better salary than many other jobs. Then, as now, politics was an issue within the police department. Politics decided who would be promoted and who would be hired; one had to have "connections" for advancement as opposed to the knowledge and qualifications required for the job. In those times, police were called *peace officers*, because their primary job was to keep the peace as opposed to fighting crime. The Boston Police Department was the first to develop the position of detective. Before then, anyone who wished to earn money could offer his services as a "bounty hunter" for others.

During this period, almost all police departments were corrupt, incompetent, and disliked by those they served. However, as police departments became more institutionalized, they began to change. Many organizations were formed to make serious efforts to educate and train police officers in the first half of this century. The International Association of Chiefs of Police (IACP) was formed, and through its work a substantial number of positive changes were made. Schools of criminology were formed where officers could be trained, and books were written on the profession of policing.

There were changes of equipment too. By 1850,

police headquarters began to communicate with precincts through the use of telegraph police boxes. In 1857 in Detroit, police officers began to use bicycles for transportation. By 1910, the first police cars were used. Police wagons followed in 1912, and 1913 saw the first use of motorcycles by police. By midcentury, policing became widely known as law enforcement, and it was modeled after the military.

In the 1960s and 1970s, policing went through yet another change, and restrictions began to be imposed on the amount of authority a police officer had while on duty on the street. In the 1980s, the police assumed another role, so that today they are not simply "enforcers of the law" but also practice "community policing."

Today, the sheriff's department serves rural areas; the metropolitan police serve the cities; and state police patrol larger areas and are most often associated with highway patrolling. Federal law enforcement agencies are umbrella organizations for a number of groups that protect the rights and privileges of all of us as United States citizens. There are agencies such as the Department of Justice, the Federal Bureau of Investigation (FBI), and the Drug Enforcement Administration (DEA). There are also private police agencies, such as the security police groups that work in malls, within stores and apartment complexes, as well as patrolling private businesses.

More personal policing by officers who know and identify with the community is in demand today. Crime is so complex, and people in large cities can feel so deprived of their individual identity, that citizens want both protection and a sense of personal identity with law enforcement persons. Of course today, both men and women work in law enforcement.

FAIRNESS OF THE COURT SYSTEM

The court system in the United States does not ask that the *accused* (the defendant, who has been charged with a crime) prove that he or she is not guilty. The system maintains that a person is innocent until proven guilty (this is called the *presumption of innocence*). Therefore, it is the responsibility of the state (or *prosecution*, representing the police, law enforcement agents, and, by extension, society at large) to prove that the accused is guilty.

The courts have been created to give all citizens a fair opportunity to present their side of the story. The courts try to reach a just conclusion, which may be either *acquittal* (the person is not guilty) or *sentencing* (the person is guilty). In a free and democratic society, respect for the law and its administrators is very important. It is a cornerstone in the building of the nation.

Decisions about the guilt or innocence of an accused person should be determined as a result of a thorough and fair judicial process. Like any process that involves human beings, this process has flaws. There are times when it is extremely difficult to determine the truth. The process does not always arrive at a just decision. There have been times when innocent people have gone to jail unjustly—or in more extreme cases, executed mistakenly—because the judicial process failed to work correctly. To help prevent such situations, all citizens should respect the judicial process and abide by a code of honesty and integrity on behalf of justice.

FROM ARREST TO SENTENCING

A person is arrested when the police believe that he or she has committed a crime, or at least when there is sufficient evidence (called *probable cause*) to detain that person. Before being taken to jail, the person is advised of his or her right to a legal defense. Usually, when a person is arrested, he or she is searched for weapons and interrogated. Basic information is required, such as name, address, telephone number, age, gender, and race. (You will remember that earlier we spoke about the requirement that arrest records be maintained and counted for the "uniform crime report.")

Following custody, if there is probable cause to charge the individual with a crime, the case is sent to the office of the prosecutor. There the crime is given a title. If it is a *misdemeanor,* which is a minor crime (often called a *complaint*), and if the accused is found guilty, punishment is usually less than one year of imprisonment.

The case could be titled a *felony,* a more serious crime for which the guilty person can be punished by serving more than one year in a state prison. Those so incarcerated can also lose the right to vote, the right to hold elective office, and other rights.

After the prosecutor has determined the nature of the crime, the case will be scheduled to be heard in either a *grand jury* or a *preliminary hearing.* Grand juries hear cases when there is some doubt about the evidence. The cases are presented by the prosecutor, and they are not conducted in public to protect the person who has been accused of the crime. The preliminary hearing is an open hearing in which the accused is read his or her rights and is then asked what plea is being submitted—guilty or not guilty.

After this, a trial date can be set, and bail may be arranged. *Bail* is money posted by the accused so that he or she may be released from jail until the time for the further judicial action. The amount of money required for bail is determined by the judge. The accused is not allowed to leave town before the trial, and the bail payment helps ensure this outcome. Persons who do leave town and "skip bail" forfeit the money, and the authorities begin an immediate search for them.

Those persons who cannot pay the bail often remain in jail until their trial, unless the judge releases them into the custody of someone who agrees to be responsible for them. Some persons will be released from jail on their own *recognizance*—promise to the court—that they will return for trial. Those persons are generally not accused of violent or serious crimes.

Plea bargaining is often a part of the process. When this takes place, the defense lawyer (the lawyer for the accused) and the prosecutor meet and attempt to settle the issue without going to trial (next section).

When an agreement cannot be reached, a trial is held before a judge or jury. Both the prosecutor and the defense lawyer present their evidence and arguments. The judge or jury must decide *beyond reasonable doubt* whether or not the person is guilty. This process is called *adjudication*. When a person is found innocent of the crime, he or she is free to go. When a jury cannot agree on a decision, they are said to be a *deadlocked* or *hung* jury. The charges may be dropped, or a new trial may be ordered.

If the person is found guilty of the charge, he or she will return to court to be sentenced. This is called the *deposition*, and the result could be imprisonment, a fine, or probation. Sometimes an individual may receive a combination of the three. Those who believe that the process was unfair may *appeal* their convictions or sentencing. This is done in an *appellate court*. If that court concludes that the case was not presented properly, the individual may be granted a new trial or released.

Courts are like the hub of a wheel because they are the center around which the criminal justice system revolves.

FEDERAL AND STATE COURT SYSTEMS

There are two primary court systems: the federal system and the state system. They are similar in that they have both trial and appellate courts.

Before we consider the court systems further or look at the role of the prosecutor and the public defender, here are a few definitions that are important to understand:

- *Jurisdiction* refers to a court's power to hear and decide a case.
- *Original jurisdiction* refers to the first court to hear a case.
- *Appellate (appeal) jurisdiction* refers to the court that can hear an appeal.
- *Moot* means that a case no longer has any legal standing.

- *Standing* means that a person must have some interest or right that is in danger of being threatened with harm.

The court system has many different arms, or branches. The process of charging, setting bail, selecting a jury, conducting the trial, sentencing, and filing appeals all takes place within the court system.

Many think that the court also provides a means by which issues can be settled in the quickest and the easiest, but also the most just way possible. However, there are those who do not agree that this is the case. They maintain that the court system is costly, slow and adversarial, and that alternatives such as mediation and arbitration might be preferable to what most often takes place.

In the court system, a defendant works with his or her attorney, who then works with the prosecutor and the judge, and they—with the defendant's consent—can agree to a lesser charge, or the defendant can agree to make restitution. There can be an alternative penalty, such as performing 100 hours of community service. These agreements are a part of plea bargaining, which we mentioned briefly in an earlier section. Plea bargaining does not always work in the best interest of all parties involved; often, those individuals who have previous records of crime benefit as much as persons who are offenders for the first time. Plea bargaining has become popular and expedient because of the serious overcrowding in the court system. In fact, there are those who believe that the courts are operating "assembly-line justice," meaning the plea-bargaining process has become automatic and there are few jury trials, because a speedy trial can no longer be obtained.

There are several court jurisdictions. Let us take a brief look at them.

Courts of general jurisdiction primarily handle serious felony cases such as robbery, rape, and murder. Some of the courts of general jurisdiction also review cases on appeal. Courts of limited jurisdiction also fall in this category. They handle such misdemeanors as writing bad checks, shoplifting, and simple assault.

Appellate courts receive defendants who believe that their rights were violated while involved in a trial. Defendants may file for an appeal if their right to due process and/or equal protection was violated. Appellate courts do not try cases; they only review them to determine whether a mistake has been made by any judicial party involved. The court can allow the defendant to go free, ask for a new trial, or uphold (maintain) the first verdict. At the state level, there are state supreme courts, which also review and make decisions regarding appeals.

U.S. district courts are trial courts for the federal system. They oversee cases that involve violations of federal laws. Examples of these cases are kidnapping and civil rights abuses. Generally, a single judge will sit in these trials, and defendants may request that a jury be selected as well. In certain very complicated civil rights cases, as many as three judges may preside over the court.

When an individual appeals from the U.S. district court, that case will be heard in the *federal appeals court,* also called the *U.S. circuit court.* In earlier times, the judges who presided over these courts had to ride horseback from one county to another and were sometimes referred to as *C.C. riders.* Of course today, judges no longer ride horseback, and very few still preside over more than one court. Circuit courts do not try cases. Instead they assess, evaluate, analyze, and interpret the law.

The *U.S. Supreme Court* is the highest appellate court in the United States. It is the end of the road for all the cases tried in the state and federal courts. The Supreme Court is the only court that was established by the U.S. Constitution, and its primary function is to apply federal laws as they are interpreted by the Constitution.

Nine justices (judges) sit on the Supreme Court. There has been only one female member of the court in history, and she is a member of the current court. Her name is Sandra Day O'Connor. Thurgood Mar-

Earlier courts, such as this one in nineteenth-century New York, were even more crowded and confused than today's hard-pressed courts. (Courtesy of The Library of Congress)

shall was the only African-American member of the court. The president appoints the justices, and the U.S. Senate confirms their appointment. A chief justice presides over the Supreme Court. The current chief justice, William H. Rehnquist, was appointed by former President Reagan.

THE ROLE OF THE JUDGE

The judge is the most senior person in a court of law. To qualify to be a judge, the individual must have extensive legal credentials, and he or she must be established as an ethical person dedicated to the equal pursuit of justice for all. Judges must instruct people on how to give evidence or how that evidence should be received, and they must also rule on what behavior is allowed in court. In some courts, the judges must direct the questioning of the witnesses and defendants and make decisions about whether or not they will find (decide) for the complainant (the one who presses charges) or for the defendant. As you might imagine, this decision making can sometimes be a very difficult, and very sad, task for judges.

Most often, judges work with a number of people who service the court, such as the police, the probation officer, the district attorney, and the court clerk. At the same time they must take great care to maintain impartial, critical thinking. Judges must be excellent leaders for they are the head of the court. Yet they should never abuse their power.

THE PROSECUTION

The prosecutor is often described as the chief law enforcer. One of the prosecutor's major functions is to charge the defendant and bring that individual to trial. The prosecutor must oversee all the processing for a given case, beginning with the arrest and continuing right up to the sentencing or appeal. Since the prosecutor functions as an attorney for the court, he or she speaks for the court whenever necessary, enforces the law, and handles plea bargaining. Additionally, the prosecutor works with the police department to investigate cases and interview witnesses.

A federal prosecutor is called a *U.S. attorney.* At the state or county level, the prosecutor is referred to as an *attorney general;* and in a city or municipality, the prosecutor is called a *district attorney.* The *U.S. attorney general* is the head of the Department of Justice.

THE DEFENSE

The accused person is defended by either a public defender or a defense attorney. Generally, a public defender is a lawyer in the government's employ who does not charge a fee to clients. A defense attorney is a private lawyer who will charge a fee to clients. In an earlier discussion about the issues of race, power, and gender, we noted that accused people who cannot afford the cost of a lawyer must be provided with the services of a public defender, assigned and paid by the court out of money from taxes.

It has been difficult to present a brief description of the U.S. court system because of its highly complex structure. Nevertheless, the important points for you to remember are very straightforward: the court system has been designed to provide due process of law for every citizen; all citizens have a constitutional right to expect fair and equal treatment before the law; and all citizens are entitled to make an appeal if they have reason to believe that they did not receive a fair review.

REVIEW QUESTIONS

1. Where did the United States get its model for policing? Do you know about policing as it is practiced in other cultures and countries?
2. What are some things that you think can be done to promote better relationships between police officers and members of the communities where they are assigned?
3. Why do you think that police officers often are viewed negatively by people in the community?
4. What comes to your mind when you hear the term *community policing*?
5. Do you think that police officers should live in the communities that they are assigned to protect?
6. What are some of the careers of people who work within the court system?
7. Can you name and briefly tell about the various courts within the judicial system?
8. What are the primary duties of the public defender?
9. Do you know how the work of the public defender differs from that of the prosecutor?

3 | History and Debate: Prisons

How were early prisons different from today's prisons?
What are reformatories?
What is the difference between a prison and a jail?
What is life like in prison?

THE HISTORY OF PRISONS

When the United States was a new nation, the punishments for crimes included public whippings, mutilations, brandings, and death. The Quakers, a religious group known for their humanitarianism, helped get laws passed that made labor the new form of punishment. The Quakers also promoted the use of prisons as the means to move away from the cruel and inhumane treatment of criminals.

The first U.S. prison was built in 1787 on Walnut Street in Philadelphia, Pennsylvania. People who broke the law were sent to this jail to pay for their crimes by working very hard and receiving no pay. Those who were in charge of the criminal justice system thought that hard labor would be just punishment and would be so severe that those who were prisoners would decide not to commit crimes again.

Whipping was punishment for violating prison rules as recently as this century. (Delaware, 1907) *(Courtesy of The Library of Congress)*

This view about the purpose of prisons is usually called a *just deserts model* (which we mentioned earlier); it is also referred to as *deterrence* and *retribution*. Furthermore, it was thought that others who might commit a crime would learn by the example of those in prison. The Walnut Street Jail soon became the model for prisons in America.

Very soon, however, the need for change in the prison system became apparent, for indeed, crimes were still being committed and more and more people began to be placed in the prisons. Even in those early times, overcrowding was a problem, and more prisons had to be built.

The Quakers continued to think about the problems of prisons. They believed that an individual who had committed a crime would benefit from *penance.* Penance is a process by which a person goes into seclusion—that is, stays away from the rest of society—thinks about what he or she did that was wrong, while seeking forgiveness. Quakers wanted a place for offenders to do penance and believed that it should provide an environment where kindness and spirituality prevailed and where no harsh and cruel punishment would be allowed. From this concept of isolation and penance, we derive the term *penitentiary.* The Quakers established the first penitentiary in 1790.

Unfortunately, the penitentiary system fared no better than the prison system. The concept of forgiveness was no better accepted than the concept and the practice of punishment. Probably because of conditions within the penitentiaries as well as in the communities where many of the crimes were committed, crimes continued and overcrowding remained a major problem.

Overcrowding meant that prisoners were forced to stay in cramped quarters and that people who were very different from one another in behavior and attitude had to live together. Overcrowding led to brutal behaviors among both the prisoners and the guards. It was evident that new ideas and new reforms needed to be developed for a more humane treatment of prisoners and for their rehabilitation.

Over time, young people became the focus of those concerned about crime. The thinking was that although adults might not be redeemable, there could be hope for youthful offenders. It was concluded that young people committed crimes primarily because they lived in conditions of poverty. A new idea emerged: to take young people, already in trouble, away from the crimes and poverty of the cities into the countryside in programs of reform and protection. These programs became known as *reformatories*. The primary purpose of the reformatories was to assist with rehabilitation or reform, so that young people could return home to be good and productive citizens.

Unfortunately, although the reformatory was a very good idea, it failed to work well. Many administrators of reformatories were dishonest and did not treat their charges fairly. Numerous youngsters were abused, both physically and mentally. Instead of reforming, many youths became hostile and bitter because of the abusive treatment they had received.

Many administrators of reformatories, penitentiaries, and prisons have thought that it was their duty to punish offenders who were placed in their care.

This idea of punishment, as opposed to rehabilitation and reform, has always had wide support from the American community.

Because of the shortcomings of reformatories, a new form of incarceration was proposed, called the *industrial prison.* Industrial prisons came into existence at the end of the Civil War, when Southern states needed to find new sources of labor after their slaves were freed. These prisons were operated like factories and used the chain-gang form of punishment. The chain gang comprised a group of prisoners, linked together by iron chains, who were forced to work in coal mines and to rebuild roads and buildings. The use of prison labor was vital to the rebuilding of the South, which had been devastated during the war. Only men were placed in chain gangs, and most of them were Black males who had once been enslaved. These men were frequently engaged in petty crime because they could find no jobs and were trying to provide for themselves and their families.

Chain gangs were also used in the North. However, those people without jobs and homes in the North were more likely to be arrested because they could not pay their bills. Those persons were then sentenced to debtors' prisons, which were really prison *workhouses.* The idea of a workhouse was that people who hadn't paid their bills would work off the debt doing enforced labor. Because of the limited number of jobs available, the debtors' prisons also became very overcrowded.

So far, we have discussed three types of imprisonment between 1790 and 1930—the prison (including the industrial prison and the workhouse), the penitentiary, and the reformatory. We have seen that overcrowding has always been a problem for prisons.

JAILS

A jail is a facility where people are detained for the following reasons: (1) they cannot pay bail or are ineligible for bail; (2) they have been convicted of a crime and are awaiting sentence; (3) they are being confined because they have committed a misdemeanor; (4) they are waiting for a hearing; (5) the state facilities are overcrowded. Some jurisdictions have lockups that keep offenders for up to forty-eight hours. Some jails, referred to as *houses of correction*, maintain people who are convicted of misdemeanors or those who have been found guilty and have been sentenced to serve up to one year in jail.

Most often, jails are managed or administered by a county sheriff who takes direction from the county board of supervisors, grand jury committee, or some form of court government. In some jurisdictions, residents of the local community are selected to be members of the grand jury committee, which may be responsible for inspecting the local jail and determining that it is run correctly. The grand jury committee or county government will be concerned about maintaining healthy, decent living conditions for the inmates. They are required to make reports to their town councils or town administrators two to three times a year.

Because most local sheriffs are elected, they have a particular motivation to do a good job of managing the jail. But good sheriffs are not just concerned about elections; they are competent and hardworking professionals dedicated to a just penal system.

Other elected officials include the judge, the district attorney (often called the *D.A.*, a term you may have heard on television). There are other legal officials who also help determine who goes to jail. Each county or community may have slightly different laws that provide guidelines on who should go to jail, and for how long. But all jails must follow the laws of the nation in accordance with the U.S. Constitution.

CEDRICK IN JAIL

Here is what happened to Cedrick, whom we met in the Introduction, within the criminal justice system.

Before Cedrick was convicted and sentenced to prison, he was detained in jail. That period of time when he was in jail was called *pretrial*. Cedrick was placed in the jail to await his trial to determine whether he was guilty of the crime of stealing a car. That crime is usually classified as "Grand Theft, Auto."

While Cedrick was in jail, he was housed in what is called a *cell block* with several other persons who were also awaiting trial. Women as well as men were imprisoned in that jail; however, they were housed in another section of the facility. In some jails, women are the cooks and do laundry for the prisoners, while the men do the heavier work. They mop the halls, clean the bathrooms, wash windows, and remove trash. Some of the women or the men who have the skills might work in the jail offices where they type letters, file documents, and answer telephones.

Cedrick's jail had a gym where prisoners could

exercise. There was also an enclosed outdoor basket-ball court. Many jails do not provide exercise facilities because they are very expensive to operate and main-tain. Jails will provide them only if they have enough money in their budgets.

Where Cedrick was in jail, prisoners could watch television in the evening for a defined period of time. Lights usually are out by 10:00 P.M. because some prisoners must be up as early as 4:30 A.M. for break-fast. Schedules in many jails are very different from what we usually think of as normal. Dinner may be as early as 3:00 P.M., and there is no bedtime snack. A count of the prisoners is taken as many as three times a day to determine how many persons are in jail and whether anyone is missing. Most criminolo-gists appear to agree that life as a prisoner, whether in jail or in prison, is dull, boring, and routine.

GOING TO PRISON

It should be noted here that not all prisons are exactly alike. They may differ from the jail in which Cedrick stayed at first. Jails differ in the amount of security imposed—that is, measures taken to keep prisoners from getting out—as well as in their restrictions on behavior. They also differ in the amount of education or rehabilitation they offer. Some prisons are called *minimum-security prisons*. They generally hold prisoners who are not thought to be violent or likely to escape, and the guards there do not have to enforce rules that are as strict as those at some other prisons. *Maximum-security prisons,* on the other hand, have walls, more guards, and many restrictions. In some cases, different sections of the same prison have different levels of security. Not only do prisons differ, but the same kinds of prisons differ from state to state.

Cedrick is serving his sentence in a typical prison. The crime of Grand Theft, Auto, carries a sentence of from one to five years of imprisonment. Because it was the first major offense for Cedrick, and because of his age and the fact that he did not have any other police record, he received a reduced sentence. He was ultimately placed in the youth correctional center within the state prison. You may remember that this was the minimum-security section of the prison. Here are the steps by which Cedrick and his fellow prisoners arrived at and got oriented to the prison facilities.

After persons have been sentenced, they are put into the custody of the Department of Corrections and held in either the county jail or the city jail until

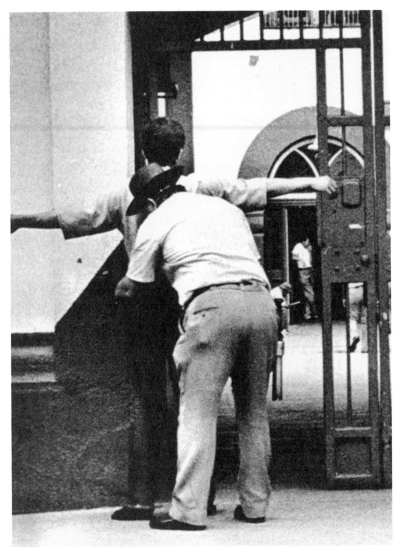

Prison security includes elaborate and unpleasant measures, such as this search for smuggled weapons. (Copyright Washington Post; *reprinted by permission of the D.C. Public Library)*

they are transported to the prison. Thus Cedrick was returned to the jail where he had awaited his trial, this time to wait to be transported in a prison bus to prison. Most prison buses have bars on their windows and are designed so that the prisoners are separated from the officers who must guard and transport them. These officers take with them the various papers that will explain to the prison authorities the details of the sentencing of each person.

When they arrive, new prisoners are given a physical examination to determine their health. They are usually required to shower and shampoo, submit to a urine analysis to determine whether they have been taking drugs, and undergo a body search for drugs and weapons. Prison clothes are then issued, and the prisoners are given the rules and regulations of the prison. They will quickly come to understand that they must obey those rules.

Certainly by this time, Cedrick understood that someone else—the prison authorities—would be making all the decisions about his life for the next several months. Cedrick and the others who arrived with him were probably placed in isolation for a period of time during which their *orientation* to the prison took place. He was given a number of tests that determined his level of education and abilities, and he was told what part of the prison he would live in, based on the type of crime of which he had been found guilty. During this orientation period, Cedrick was not allowed to have visitors, and his phone calls were limited.

The prison authorities explained to Cedrick that his mail might be read by authorities during his time in prison, and he was told what things he would be allowed to have with him in his prison residence. A list of those items, which are called *allowables*, can be found in the Appendix.

As we have said, life in prison is routine and often boring. In prison, people are deprived of their individualism. These are some of the ways this happens: prisoners cannot wear their own clothes (in most instances); they can have only a very limited number of personal belongings (primarily items for grooming and health, such as comb and brush, deodorant, toothbrush, toothpaste; they are not allowed any privacy at any time; they are told what time to rise, shower, play, eat, put the light out, go to bed. This form of prison life is the same for both men and women, young and old, with a few exceptions.

RULES AND REGULATIONS

A prison is a small community. Within the prison there are particular patterns of behavior, judged acceptable or unacceptable, for which there is either reward or sanction. There is even a prison language, used by the correctional officers, the administrators, and the inmates.

New prisoners must learn the folkways and the mores—the formal and the informal rules—of the prison. After they have lived in prison for some time, persons most often adjust to that environment and begin to "feel at home." This acceptance of prison life is called *becoming institutionalized* or *prisonized* because the individual is learning to function within the life-style of the prison.

Every part of life in prison is regulated. Here are some examples of what inmates may be told:

- how clean they must keep their living quarters
- where they can and cannot wear certain clothing
- how many visitors they may receive and when they may be visited
- to carry identification cards at all times
- when and how they may purchase items from the prison store.

Many more rules and regulations appear in the prison instructions, which are excerpted in the Appendix.

Some people become so prisonized that upon release, they find they cannot function in the outside world; they have become completely used to being told how to live their lives. Studies have reported that some prisoners become so dependent on the structure of the prison that after they are released and returned to their communities, they deliberately commit a crime in order to be returned to prison. This is most likely to happen to persons who return to a community where they are not well accepted and not given the support of family and loved ones.

REHABILITATION: SCHOOL AND WORK

While he is in prison, Cedrick has to work and go to school. If he applies himself to his studies, he will be able to learn a trade, finish his work for his high school degree, and even begin college courses. For Cedrick and the other young men who are imprisoned, there are also classes in such areas as theater, music, photography, art, and writing. All these educational programs are intended to encourage the prisoners to become prepared for positive, gainful em-

Vocational training has been a feature of prisons for a century. In 1915, Sing Sing inmates learned the trade of knitting. (Courtesy of The Library of Congress)

ployment when they return to their communities. The program for education is part of a larger rehabilitation program. It has been documented that the large majority of prisoners in jails, prisons, and penitentiaries are people who dropped out of school at an early age for a range of reasons. And as you know, without a good education and knowledge of modern technical skills, it is virtually impossible to have access to the best jobs.

Many prisons employ inmates for work within the prison at less than minimum wage. Prisoners work at various jobs ranging from laundry work to making license plates to tailoring or furniture upholstering. Often there is not enough work for all prisoners to work a full eight-hour day. Private businesses have recently become involved in prison industries, where they employ prisoners at wages somewhat lower than those in the community. This is part of a process known as the *privatization*—business for profit by private companies—of the prisons. Data processing and microfilming are two areas where private companies have had some success inside the prisons.

Although prisoners begin work at minimum wages in these programs, as they become more skilled they may receive a raise. Should the prisoners not perform at the level expected, they are fired, just as if they were working in the outside world.

To become employees in such a program, prisoners must go through a screening process. Unfortunately, the average inmate has not completed high school, and many have not had a good employment record. Therefore, only a few prisoners pass the employment screening interview. For example, a data processing company located in a Minnesota prison employs a total of only twenty inmates out of many hundreds imprisoned there.

PRISON COSTS

At this time, there are more than 450,000 people in prisons in the United States. The total population of those imprisoned in prisons and jails is 771,243, or 293 people per 100,000. The number of juveniles imprisoned is 52,123. The number of inmates is steadily growing, and overcrowding continues to be a serious problem for all incarceration facilities. But building new prisons is not as simple as it may sound. Because of the services that they must provide and the requirements of security, prisons are expensive to build. When we build prisons, we build small communities. First, there must be a transportation service to get prisoners to and from the prisons. Also, within the prisons there must be infirmaries for those who become ill or need medical assistance; kitchens to prepare food for the large number of people and a dining space where people eat; a power plant for electricity; a sewage disposal unit; buildings or locations where labor can be learned and performed; and areas for the prison school.

In addition, there must be many prison guards, counselors, correctional officers, teachers, instructors, supervisors, doctors, nurses, secretaries, administrators, and wardens—all of whom help maintain or operate the prison. Of course, all these people must be paid. Their salaries come from taxes paid by citizens like you and your parents. As the communities become larger and larger, the expenses increase

San Francisco's Alcatraz Island held the federal government's most infamous prisoners. (Courtesy of The Library of Congress)

and additional taxes are required in order to pay the staff.

Some prisons have farms on which they produce food. In those situations, additional money will be required for the purchase of tractors, trucks, tools, and modern farming equipment. And if there is livestock, more money will have to be set aside for the animals' food and shelter.

Generally, when people talk about the costs of a prison, they speak about *bed costs*, that is, the amount of money that will be required to maintain one prisoner sleeping in one bed for which there must be all the resources we have mentioned. The bed-cost figure used today is approximately $25,000 per year, or as much as it costs to send you or one of your classmates to an Ivy League university or college for one year.

Because construction costs have risen, some prison experts suggest that the price to build a prison will soon increase to as much as $72,000 to $100,000 total costs per bed (person) per year. These costs will continue to increase as more people are needed to maintain the prison system and as those who work there demand more pay to compensate for the alleged dangers involved in their jobs.

From the discussion in this chapter, we can conclude that there are a number of reasons we put people in prison:

- to punish them
- to rehabilitate them so they can return to their communities
- to protect the public safety

- to have them serve as an example that will deter others from committing crimes.

Some of those in favor of prisons stress their punitive nature, taken to the extreme in cases of capital punishment. Others focus more on the role of prisons in reform and rehabilitation. Both these groups consider prisons—despite their considerable shortcomings—to be the best solution we have found to date in dealing with the ongoing problem of crime in America. But another group sees prisons as increasingly ineffective and advocates alternatives to imprisonment. This debate will be discussed more fully in Chapter 5, but first, let's turn our attention to juvenile offenders and to those young people who have ties with someone in prison.

REVIEW QUESTIONS

1. What do you think Cedrick would tell us about his prison experience?
2. Do you think that people who commit crimes because they are addicted to drugs (remember that alcohol is a drug) should be imprisoned?
3. What is the main feature of life in prison?
4. How have prisons changed over the years? Have they changed for the better?
5. How has work in prison changed over the years? Has it changed for the better?
6. Has building more and more prisons for more and more people solved the problem of crime?
7. Do you think there are solutions to crime other than prisons?

8. How do you think that some prisoners could be encouraged to study and learn skills that would prepare them to work in the private prison programs, as well as for companies on the outside after their release?
9. Do you think that it is a good idea for private businesses to be able to operate within prisons, where they can hire prisoners for less than the going wages on the outside, but more than the wages paid by the prison for work?

4 Young People, Families, and Friends

Why do people join gangs?
What do some gangs have to do with crime?
Are young offenders different from adult criminals?
How does the criminal justice system deal with young people?
What it is like to visit a friend in prison?
What does life hold for someone returning from prison?

THE JUVENILE OFFENDER

As we have seen, dealing with young people who commit crimes in the United States led to the creation of the juvenile justice system and the establishment of reformatories. In the 1960s it became apparent, however, that many children involved in the criminal justice system were not being given their legal rights. Through two cases brought before the U.S. Supreme Court (Kent and Gault), the juvenile justice system was reformed. It became an advocate for children, and most important, it began to focus on *crime prevention*.

Prevention is an action taken to deter or to correct harmful situations or antisocial behavior, that is, behavior against the community. Prevention is often linked to the juvenile system because there is a strong desire to "protect" children and youth from any harm, whether it be at home, on the streets, among other children, or self-harm.

Children become part of the juvenile justice system for a number of reasons: (1) they have no parent, guardian, or other adult who is responsible for their guidance; (2) they are being abused or are highly likely to be abused by someone; or (3) they are in emotional distress and need professional help.

Some children are called *throw-away children* because they have been abandoned by their parents. They have no place to live. Many children and youths in this situation are placed in youth homes, foster care homes, or a community treatment program.

There are also children who act out anger, hostility, frustrations, and various other feelings through behaviors that are offensive or harmful to other people or property. They are called *juvenile delinquents*. Usually their offenses are minor; however, sometimes they cause serious injury to themselves or others, or violate the law. Some damage property. Some threaten other children or take money from them; or they steal items from a store or a person. They may think such behavior is daring, brave, or fun.

If this behavior is discovered, they will be arrested, taken into custody, arraigned, and forced to undergo the rest of the judicial process. You may know someone who has been involved with the police and, as a result, in the juvenile justice system. In the system they are known as *adjudicated juveniles*. Some of them may be sent to detention centers for rehabilitation or for discipline. Some of them may be sent to other facilities or to foster homes because their parents can no longer control them. Still other children or youths might be placed in counseling, with a probation office. If the last action is taken, they are most likely to be in a program called *Person in Need of Service (PINS)*. Some are referred to the PINS program by their families or by their school.

More persons under the age of eighteen are arrested each year. Today, juvenile courts hear about one million offense cases and 400,000 reported child abuse cases a year. Substance abuse, most often abuse of alcohol, is a significant factor in 60 to 90 percent of all cases. Many young people are frequent users of drugs other than alcohol, and a large number of them have committed violent crimes, which makes them subject to harsher punishment within the juvenile justice system.

When juveniles are taken into custody today, they are placed as quickly and appropriately as possible. Detention centers are used to house those who are awaiting decisions from the juvenile court. There are also diagnostic centers for those youths ordered to undergo intensive evaluations and assessments prior to placement in a correctional facility.

Facilities for juveniles include training schools, camps, and ranches. Training schools are considered to be more secure (they restrict the movements and privileges of their residents more) than are the camps and ranches located in the countryside. There are also group homes where more than one juvenile might live. These homes are managed by counselors who live on the same premises as the juveniles.

_By law, courts must provide public defenders for those who
cannot afford a lawyer._ (Courtesy of The Library of Congress)

Additionally, there are family group homes. Of all arrangements, the preferred setting is a foster home, in which the juvenile receives proper attention and care from a nurturing family.

Even though every attempt is made to house juveniles in facilities designed for them, approximately 250,000 to 300,000 juveniles are held in adult jails. As many as 25 percent of those juveniles are accused of truancy and running away from home. These minor infractions are called *status offenses,* and about 75 percent of those in jail on such charges will be released after their court hearing. Regrettably, any time spent in jail can be very harmful to juveniles, some of whom are so disturbed by this experience that they attempt suicide.

This inappropriate detention of juveniles is indicative of a juvenile justice system that has not followed through on its original promise: to act in the best interest of the child. Children are not necessarily granted due process—basic rights—and many have found themselves in difficult situations through no fault of their own. Since the children of a society are its future citizens, and its greatest asset, continued attention must be given to evaluating and improving the juvenile justice system.

WHAT IS A GANG?

We have said that some people commit crimes because they want to impress a group to which they belong. Remember that Cedrick had formed a strong friendship with a group that considered crime acceptable.

Many different types of gangs exist, and they are

formed for many different reasons. The composition of a gang is variable—for example, all members might be adults, or others have only youngsters, or women, or men. People come together in gangs because they have a common bond. They share an attitude, behavior, or belief around which they can unite (even though they may differ in many ways). They like the other members of the gang, and they especially like the sense of belonging that the gang provides. Gangs can be good or bad, and certainly not all gangs are involved in crimes.

In many ways, a gang operates like any club. Just as a club has officers, such as the president and vice president, a gang uses various ranks of importance, such as the leader and other members of the leadership group. In a club, members become leaders because the general membership knows that they have a particular skill or ability. The president of the club, for example, might be a good speaker or a person who is very popular. The leader of the gang might also be a good speaker or one who can persuade others. Without a doubt, the leader will be a person who has convinced the group of his or her loyalty.

Experts who study street gangs tell us that they give young people a sense of identity, belonging, power, security, and discipline—five reasons that gangs can be so appealing. Unique names, particular colors or color combinations, and secret codes and symbols are aspects of gang life that provide a sense of identity, as well as a taste of adventure and excitement.

The feeling of belonging that a gang provides is especially appealing to young people who are idle, who are poor students, or who have been alienated—

that is, left out—and feel they do not "fit in." For some young people, their street gang is the only group where they feel a strong attachment to others. The gang, like a school club, gives them a place to go and something to do with their free time that makes them feel they belong and are important.

The sense of power results from the gang's ability to be successful with the goals it has set. Many have observed that television, movies, and news reports contribute to the members' view of themselves as "tough" and "threats" to the community.

The sense of security provided by gangs could come both from "belonging" and from the protection that gang members provide for one another. In many places, especially in overcrowded parts of large cities, neighborhoods where young people live are carved out into territories, or *turf*, that different gangs rule. Many young people have reported that in order to avoid harassment, one simply joins one gang or the other.

Gangs who are involved in illegal activities have a greater need to protect their members. For safety's sake, they must demand strict discipline within the group, and the leadership must be firm and consistent.

Criminal gangs can be found in any community. However, those gangs which are most often kept under strict police surveillance are most likely to be located in poor communities. To understand this, you will need to remember what we said about the role of prejudice in the formation of attitudes about who commits crimes.

It is also important to remember that many young people join criminal gangs to gain illegal material things, as well as for status and the other reasons we have mentioned. Gang membership for money or material things is often the result of the low incomes of their families—particularly families where the mother is the only parent in the home. We know that women are often paid lower wages for work than men are, even when it is the same exact work. This underpayment to women who are the only source of their family income results in a poverty which is known as the *feminization of poverty.*

Many young people need a chance to do meaningful work and earn at least a minimum wage. Like you, other young people feel good about themselves when they are able to buy nice things with money they have earned on their own. You can understand how important minimum wage employment is to young people from homes suffering from the feminization of poverty. Also, to deter young people from joining criminal gangs, they must have the chance to enjoy positive recreational experiences, such as belonging to groups with constructive goals and participating in programs where there are opportunities for achievement and recognition.

GANGS, DRUGS, AND CRIME

Unlike the school club and other private organizations for youth, the gang involved in crime presents a danger to the entire community. Historically, criminal gangs have participated in acts of violence. Just as in the past, gangs today commit acts of violence that result in the destruction of property. Often they are also involved in violence that results in injury or death of members as well as of innocent victims.

If you have listened to the news lately, or if you have read any of the newsmagazines or the newspapers, you know that certain gangs are involved in major crimes such as murder. Some of these gangs are very large, and they are organized into "chapters," or subgroups of members, in locations throughout the United States. Other gangs have smaller membership and operate within smaller areas. A recent study reports that one half of all crimes are committed by youth who are likely to be gang members.

Most of the news about gang activities today centers on drugs. The production, distribution, and sale of drugs is a primary source of income for many gangs, both adult and youth. Drugs are big business in America. Because there is so much money involved in illegal drugs and because the production and distribution of drugs requires connections between several different locations, some gangs have become well organized. They are structured exactly like big business.

Although numerous youth gangs are involved in illegal drugs, it is speculated that their top leaders are adults. As one national expert on gangs has said, "Granted, these groups do have large number of youth in their rank, but nonetheless their hierarchies are undeniably predominated by adult leadership. This phenomenon makes it difficult to differentiate between youth groups and adult groups."

Those gangs that are involved in crime are especially appealing to young people who want to seem tough or important, or to get things they cannot afford. They must learn that gangs are not their only option. There is a critical need for programs that provide alternative opportunities for these young people.

WHAT IF SOMEONE YOU KNOW IS IMPRISONED?

Visiting with family or friends who are imprisoned is very difficult. We have seen that most prisons are located far from major cities. So it may take considerable planning, time, and money to make the trip.

Before visiting a relative or friend in prison, ask your parent or the adult who will be taking you there to tell you what to expect when you arrive. Try to learn the rules for the visit, so that you will not get overly nervous or upset.

It can be very frightening to visit a prison. Almost everybody finds it difficult to undergo the security checks by guards who admit visitors. Sometimes the guards make visitors feel as if they are suspect themselves. If you begin to feel resentful, you will take these feelings with you into the visitor's room. Since you do not want to do that, try to think of the previsit security check as a routine measure that is not directed against you personally.

Even with this in mind, you might find it hard not to feel sad when you enter the visitor's room. The previsit check might remind you of the security as well as the restrictions, routine, and regulations under which the person you love must live. You might think that all of this security is not necessary for you and your family or friends. But you need to remember that the citizens who are victimized by crimes want to know that those who are imprisoned will not escape from the prison or jail.

You will be lucky if, like Cedrick's mother, you visit a facility where you are able to make direct contact with the prisoners. If possible, give the person you are visiting a strong, warm hug, and even a kiss if that person is very dear to you. You may be a little shy at first because it can feel strange to be warm and loving in such a public place. If you haven't seen each other recently, the imprisoned person may be surprised at how much you have grown and may simply want to have a good look at you. Family members always seem to want to do that anyway.

Do not feel shy because there are other people in the room. They will probably have little time to pay attention to you. Their visit is for a limited time just as yours is, and they also want to talk and spend time together with their loved one as much as they can.

If you are visiting a close family member, such as a parent or brother or sister, remember that even though your relative is in prison, he or she still loves you and misses you. Your relative's happiness at seeing you might lead to an outburst of tears. There is also a strong possibility that the adult who has brought you to visit will also start to cry. He or she is sad because the person you are visiting has to be in prison, but happy to have even the brief time to spend together. Emotions can be very confusing at such times. Do not be embarrassed by your feelings. Hugs, a strong embrace, a kiss, a strong handshake— all help you and your family say that you care and that you are happy to be able to visit.

It is important for parents and adults to take children to visit their family in prison; however, it is also a time when the adults need to talk about many important things. You might have to wait your turn while other members of your group are visiting, because there are restrictions on the number of visitors at a given time. If you are present when parents are visiting, you will want to stay near and yet allow them some time to talk. Try to just be yourself and do what the adults ask you, even if it means allowing them to talk privately for a while. If they talk too long, you might go over and remind them that you are there because you care about the person you are visiting and want to be near. When plans are made for the next visit, you might remind the adults that you want to be included in part of the visit and that you do not want to spend most of your time sitting around while the adults talk.

Try to understand that visits are difficult because of the distance and expense involved. When you are unable to visit frequently, it is very important for you to think of other ways to keep in touch.

*For inmates and their families, visiting times are a respite from
the lonely, harsh routine of prison life.* (Copyright Washington
Post; *reprinted by permission of the D.C. Public Library*)

STAYING IN TOUCH

Persons in prison have told us that they like to receive letters that share news about you and other people they know. You should write about your activities and your plans for the future. Write about what is going on among family and friends in your community. Tell about the things you like to do, and if you have a problem and need advice you can also write about that.

When you mail your letter, be sure that you have the complete and correct address. If necessary, have an adult family member check it for you. Include photographs of yourself, your friends, some activity you are involved in (a photo of you at bat or in a school activity). This is a good time for you to become a photo buff. A book of photos would make a very nice surprise gift for a relative in prison. Be sure to write on the back of the photos and identify people your relative might not know. For example, you might write "This is Joe, my best friend."

You might also want to send by mail a picture that you drew at home or at school or a special card that you made. Remember that you can send a card if you do not want to write a letter. Many funny cards and special-message cards are widely available today, so you do not have to wait for a birthday or a holiday to send one.

Clippings and articles from newspapers and magazines make interesting mail. Perhaps you have read something that you think will be of interest to the person in prison, or you want to make sure that that person knows about an issue of political and social importance. You can also send entire books and magazines, which will help the individual keep current. You will need to ask about the prison's rules for mail. In the Appendix of this book, we have included some of the rules and regulations so that you have an example to guide you. Keep in mind, however, that different institutions have different rules and that rules also vary by state.

Many families are protective of persons in prison because they do not want to add to their distress. They think persons in prison should not hear about the problems of family members. However, when we talked to fathers and mothers who are imprisoned, they told us that they want to know about their children's problems as well as the fun in their lives. Your family member in prison can write to you and make suggestions, and if you are having very serious problems, he or she can seek counseling through the prison resources and then be of some help to you. Your relative in prison does not want to be shut out of your life, but rather to share in what you are doing. This can be accomplished if you communicate through letters.

Sending pictures of the older people in your family is also important. The person in prison needs to know that certain family members are growing older. Then, upon release, that person will be less surprised when meeting older people for the first time after a long separation. Just as pictures show how you are growing and maturing, pictures show how the elderly are growing older.

You cannot make calls from your home to a person in prison. If there is an emergency, you may call the prison's main number and ask the prison operator to connect you to a prison authority. That person can assist you and will probably pass on your message.

When a person in prison phones home, it will probably be a collect call. If it is a social call, when family and friends are gathered and everyone wants to speak, it might help if you say who will be talking before that person speaks over the phone. Being away from the family and the community might cause the person in prison to forget the names of persons who are not immediate family. You might want to say, "My friend Clara who lives next door wants to say hello," and then let Clara speak. If you have younger sisters and brothers or there are other young children who want to talk on the telephone, you might help them save time by suggesting what to say—at least to get the conversation rolling. For example, you might say to a younger child, "This is Uncle Joe; tell him hello and your name and what you did today."

Small packages to promote cheer and to say that you are thinking about the person in prison will certainly be welcome. Again, there are very strict rules about what can be sent in packages to the prison, and you will need to check the rules. In the appendix we have included a copy of rules and regulations about family visits, the use of the mail for letters and packages, and other issues.

COMING HOME

As we have said, there are several different conditions under which a family member may return home from prison, including a program of work-release, parole, or the conclusion of a sentence served. Whatever the circumstance, the return home is not easy for the person who has been in prison or for the family.

Many members of the family and many members of the community may not want a person who is known to have been in prison to return home. Some people will be frightened or worried that the person will commit a crime again, and that the crime will be against them. Others believe that anyone who goes to prison ought to be kept there and never allowed to leave. As you certainly know by now, there are a range of attitudes about persons who commit crimes. Most of them are not helpful to those who wish to make a fresh start in life after having paid their debt to society. Let us think about some questions that might be going through the mind of a young person who is expecting a close family member to return home.

What do I tell my friends? The answer is, tell them the truth. The family member was found guilty of a crime, served a sentence in prison, and is now about to return home. You might explain that the person would not be released if the authorities did not think that there was some change in his or her attitude and behavior. You are under no obligation to tell those who are curious the personal details about the crime that was committed. Nor should you feel that you owe anyone an explanation if questions are asked about what the person will do now; you might simply state that the person has gotten more education or has learned a skill that will be helpful in gaining employment in the community.

If you have friends who tease you or who do not want to associate with you because a person in your family is returning from prison, try to explain to them some of the things we have discussed. If they insist on teasing you, speak to your parents, teacher, or adults you trust and ask them for assistance in dealing with those particular individuals.

How should I act? You are both probably going to feel a little strange and awkward. After all, it has been some time since you were together. It might be that your returning relative will want to tell you how he or she feels about the crime that was committed and talk to you about hopes for the future. Your relative might really need you to listen and to try to understand. Most of all, your relative will need to be assured of your love and your faith in his or her ability to return to a positive life. You should make it clear that you will help in any way you can, but that you do not expect your relative to do anything that will in any way violate parole (if this is the case) or that will put the freedom of family members in jeopardy. So that everyone will understand and be supportive, you might want to discuss the conditions of parole.

On the other hand, your returning relative might not want to talk about prison—in order to try to forget this experience as soon as possible. If you ask questions he or she does not want to answer, stop right there! Wait until another time, when your relative might open up to you about prison.

How the individual feels will soon be apparent. Just wait and see. Both of you will need to give each other time.

What can I do to help? Since you are not an adult, there are limits to what you can do about the more serious issues, such as finding a job and reestablishing links with the community. Of course, you might mention any jobs that you know about or you might help by looking through the newspaper for jobs. Most important, you should realize that it is very difficult to find a job after one has been in prison.

To help with the adjustment to community life, you can talk about the changes that may have taken place: give the names of the local officials, the new neighbors, and whatever persons might be involved in illegal activities (if there is such suspicion). You can try to get the person involved in some community activity or organization right away. This involvement will help foster new friendships and will also demonstrate to community members that the person intends to contribute to society in a positive way.

How should I feel? It is not unusual for you to have mixed emotions about a person whom you love who has done something that is a disappointment to you. You may feel both happy and sad at the same time, and you may wonder if your relative is really willing to avoid getting into trouble again. Do not force positive feelings. It will take some time for you to develop trust again. The person returning to the family will understand this because he or she will have attended some sessions in the prison designed to help anticipate some of your feelings. Although this can be an awkward time, be honest and *talk about your feelings.*

There will be less awkward times and less tension among those families who have kept up the closest contact. Most often, those families will have made plans for the returning family member. They and some of the parole officials may have assisted in finding employment for the ex-offender. Some lucky persons are even able to return to their previous jobs. Many employees offer work to ex-offenders when they understand that they have participated in the prison rehabilitation and education programs.

If the person in your family is returning home

without a job, you will need to provide encouragement. It might take some time before work is found. In that case, try to get your relative actively involved in work at home, such as making needed repairs, or in a hobby or in other constructive uses of time when not job hunting.

Sometimes persons returning home from prison may place a special value on privacy and quiet. After serving time in a strict environment where there is never any privacy, they may want to have "space" to themselves. They may want to shut the door more often and may enjoy spending some time alone. You might suggest simple activities we take for granted, such as a walk in the evening or a bus ride across town and back. Other suggestions for entertainment include taking out books from the library and joining a video club to catch up on good films. You will help your family member feel comfortable and secure if you spend time together and if you are happy to be seen out together in the community.

What about the rest of the family? Each member of the family will have to establish a personal relationship with the returning person. You cannot make anybody behave in any particular way. Just as you are determining how you feel and how you can be supportive, so is every other family member, including the person who is returning home. If the adjustment becomes especially difficult, going to a counselor who has special training in this area can be of assistance. It is important for people to recognize and admit when things are not going well so that they can receive counseling and assistance.

What if things go wrong again? Ultimately, the person who returns home from prison to family and community must be determined to succeed with a new life. That person must decide not to repeat the behavior that resulted in imprisonment. Although family and friends should be supportive, *the responsibility to succeed rests primarily with the ex-offender.*

In general, the public is not favorably disposed to ex-offenders, and most ex-offenders return to an economic situation that has declined considerably. Despite these and many other strikes against them, offenders must find ways to personally cope, to live within the conditions of his or her parole release, and to regain the trust and support of many members of the community as well as of family and close friends. Most of this will require very hard work, good self-discipline, and a serious change in attitudes and resources within the community.

Returning from prison is not easy. In the next chapter, we will talk about alternatives to prison. We will also discuss the impact of imprisonment on individuals and the potential for reform, rehabilitation, and a good life.

REVIEW QUESTIONS

1. Do you think that a program that teaches everyone about the criminal justice system could prevent crime?
2. What are some things that you could say to a friend of yours who is already getting into "trouble"?
3. What are some actions that could be taken in your neighborhood to prevent juvenile crime?

4. How are juvenile and adult systems of justice different, and in what ways are they the same?
5. What are some of the reasons that young people join criminal gangs? What measures might be taken by noncriminal clubs and groups (gangs) to attract members?
6. What is the feminization of poverty? How might it be ended?
7. Describe several positive youth activities in your neighborhood.
8. Do you belong to a club, an organization, or a gang? If yes, why did you join and what is the difference among these groups?

5 The Future of Criminal Justice

Do prisons stop crime?
What has overcrowding done to prisons?
What are some alternatives to prison?
What can you do about preventing crime?

HOW SUCCESSFUL ARE PRISONS?

Getting back to Cedrick, you may be wondering whether he will have been rehabilitated before returning home. Will he be able to demonstrate that he has "learned his lesson" and will not violate the law again? Will Cedrick be able to say that the prison experience was successful? Whether prisons are successful or not depends very much on the view of the individual.

Remember that some believe imprisonment must be done to protect the public from those who commit crimes, while others believe it is supposed to rehabilitate criminals. Lately, it has been observed that less emphasis is placed on rehabilitation. Many experts no longer believe that rehabilitation can be accomplished with prisons as they are today. It is said that the prison system "warehouses" inmates for longer and longer periods, but does not rehabilitate them. Many experts also worry about the increase in *recidi-*

vism. Recidivism is the returning to prison of a former inmate because he or she has committed a new crime or violated the conditions of release. With such evidence that prisons may not work to reform prisoners, it becomes more difficult to maintain programs that could promote their rehabilitation.

During the 1970s many people believed if we were to stop building prisons we would have to develop alternatives, such as community-based treatment programs. These people also believed that decent employment opportunities outside prison would help prevent recidivism, as well as prevent crime in the first place. The motto for a group called the Moratorium on Prison Construction was "Jobs, Not Jails."

With the increase in substance abuse in recent years, the rate of imprisonment has increased, thus making it necessary to build additional prisons and jails. In fact, as communities began to worry about drug dealers who took over their neighborhoods and

Prison employees, such as this prison guard, face stressful, difficult jobs. *(Copyright* Washington Post; *reprinted by permission of the D.C. Public Library)*

grew more afraid of drug-related crime, there emerged a public demand that more and more prisons be built. Many people are responding to the terrible conditions associated with drugs by saying, "Lock 'em up and throw away the key."

There is little information, to date, to show that the criminal activity associated with increased drug abuse in America is seriously decreased by simply locking up the guilty parties, unless addicted persons are counseled and treated for their drug abuse. Many persons who are addicted did not intend to become criminals, but committed crimes because their addiction required more and more money. What is hoped is that prison will correct this cycle of behavior.

Furthermore, many drugs contribute to irrational and aggressive behavior. Though addiction must not be accepted as an excuse for violence and crimes, there appears to be a need for citizens to give more serious attention to treating addicts. Attention must also be directed toward the many conditions—such as poverty, unemployment, lack of quality education, and decent housing—that help promote addiction. Many national experts, including criminologists, public policy experts, sociologists, psychologists, elected officials and other leaders, are now conducting serious discussions and analysis of this range of issues.

PUNISHMENT VERSUS REHABILITATION

Cedrick is about to return to his family and home. He has completed his prison term and is now on parole. This will be a difficult time for Cedrick; we know that parole is not easy, that Cedrick will have to live a very disciplined life, and that he cannot afford to make many mistakes.

Sometimes we refer to the prison system as a *correctional system.* Something (Cedrick's criminal behavior) or someone (Cedrick) has been corrected. Has the discipline of prison life been a positive factor in Cedrick's life? What if Cedrick felt that he was unjustly punished? What if he then became angry and did something else that was wrong? Would the prison have done its job in that case? If Cedrick were not "corrected," would that mean he or the prison failed?

Cedrick was in jail while he awaited trial. When he was found guilty, he was sent to prison. That is the typical story of someone who has committed a crime, but at both times, there were alternatives to the treatment he received.

PROBATION AND PAROLE

Probation and parole are two distinctly different alternatives to prison. They are used by the criminal justice system for three reasons: (1) to decrease overcrowding in the prisons, (2) to reward good behavior by those who are imprisoned, or (3) to provide a way to control and supervise those who are not imprisoned because they have committed a lesser crime.

Probation is a sentence. It does not involve imprisonment, but it does impose control over the behaviors and activities of an individual who is guilty of a lesser crime. For example, a person may be required to maintain a job, give up substance abuse, and not associate with known or suspected criminals. Under the rules of probation, the individual must visit a probation officer on a regular basis for evaluation and

counseling about his or her progress and to check on whether the terms of probation are being met. The probation officer will also be concerned that the individual establish or return to a stable, supportive home.

Parole is early release from prison, earned by a prisoner after he or she has served part of the sentence. The average stay in prison is generally less than half the original sentence. Most prisoners do not serve their full sentence because they have been awarded time off for good behavior, or what is called *good time*. Prisoners gain good time by behaving in a "good" manner. This means that they must obey all the rules and volunteer for such projects as donating blood or participating in medical or psychological experiments. Another good-time behavior is to attend school and do particularly well.

After release, a parolee remains under supervision

for the remainder of the official sentence. For example, a prisoner who was sentenced to three years might be released on good time after being incarcerated for only twenty-four months. That individual would be on supervised parole for the remaining twelve months of the original sentence.

As with probation, the person on parole is required to remain alcohol and drug free, to be gainfully employed (or perhaps become a student), and to establish or reside in a stable, positive home. Additionally, that individual is also expected to choose friends and associates with good character, to avoid persons who are involved in criminal activity, to stay away from areas where known criminal activity takes place, and to report to his or her parole officer on a regular basis.

Frequently, parole and probation officers instruct such persons to attend regular meetings or rehabilitation groups such as Alcoholics Anonymous (AA) or Narcotics Anonymous (NA). Parolees might also be expected to obtain regular professional counseling. Many persons are required to make restitution, that is, to pay back the victims of their crimes. This can be done through community service or through some type of "helping" work agreed upon by the judge, the attorneys, the victims, and the offender. When it is financially possible, some offenders are asked to repay the victim monetarily.

The support of family and friends, so important during imprisonment, is vital for those on probation and parole. Because the individual must not associate with criminals who may have been part of his or her group when the crime was committed, it might be very difficult to establish new friendships.

OTHER ALTERNATIVES

There are persons and organizations who believe that the continued building of jails and prisons does not stop crime. They believe that the alternatives to prisons are better, that imprisonment should come about only as a last resort, and that sentences should be shorter. Among the alternatives to prison, aside from probation and parole, are the following:

Pretrial release is the release of a person based on that person's own reputation. It is often referred to as *ROR* (released on own recognizance). This means that the person does not have to wait in jail for a trial, which relieves overcrowding in prisons, and helps keep persons who are innocent of crime from ever spending time in jail.

Third-party release is much like pretrial release. It consists of the release of a person to an organization or agency that will be responsible for that person until the trial. Again, this keeps people who may not be guilty out of jail and helps prevent overcrowding. It also allows organizations outside the traditional criminal justice system to become involved.

If a person is found guilty of a crime, there are alternative methods of punishment. These alternatives are usually suggested for those who commit less serious crimes. In *victim restitution*, people convicted of crimes who have some financial resources can reimburse the victim. In some states, criminals who make money from telling their story in a book or movie are required to give that money to the victims of the crime. In *community service*, people may be required to give a certain number of hours in service to the victim or to the community. White-collar criminals may even be required to use the talents with which they committed crimes for community service. For example, someone who used a computer to steal money from a bank may be ordered to help a community group computerize some of its operations.

Another form of incarceration, being tried in only a few states, is the *boot camp* for young offenders. Convicted offenders (many of whom have committed drug-related offenses) are sent to camps that resemble the army's training camps, which stress discipline, teamwork, and individual responsibility. People who favor this approach say that the young offenders do not come in contact with older criminals, and this is similar to the reformatory argument discussed earlier. At present, the programs are new, so it is difficult to judge their effectiveness.

Recently, a few states have experimented with restricting convicted offenders to their homes. This is reminiscent of the *house arrest* experienced by some political prisoners overseas. It is more humane than prison, because the offender can have a normal life in some ways, but he or she has no freedom outside the home. The offender is monitored by an electronic device that tells the authorities his or her whereabouts, or by frequent telephone calls to his or her home. This is a controversial alternative to prison, because many people believe it has no place in a free and democratic society. It looks too much like governmental monitoring of ordinary citizens. Because it is new, little information is available on its effectiveness. Experiments of this kind may well continue, as advances in electronic technology make them easier to implement.

IS THERE A BETTER WAY?

Some ask, are prisons serving any purpose at all? We do know that as a society, we are less tolerant of those who continue to commit criminal acts. We are also a more fearful society, as we watch the crime rate escalate year after year. We continue to lock up offenders because we believe they should be punished. Many say that the public safety is the first and greatest priority. This group believes that those who break the rules of society should not go unpunished.

We also know that prisons do deter some persons from committing crimes, and some ex-offenders from committing more crimes. We know that the prison system does stop those offenders who would continue to commit crimes, and that prisons do rehabilitate some offenders and return them to society as productive, healthy, law-abiding citizens. Obviously, if we believe all this, we will want to continue to build more prisons.

Those who believe that society is "warehousing" human beings in prison often make the criticism that such a practice is inhumane. They believe that alternatives are less costly and more effective in serving the needs of both the offender and the public. One such organization has stated, "For every person who goes to prison, two people don't go to college." And we have noted that another group chants, "Jobs, Not Jails."

Some say that prisons are not a bad idea, but the prisons we have are not effective. If the purpose of the prison system or the correctional system is to correct, perhaps the prisons should simply do a better job in the rehabilitation of prisoners. This would require making improvements in prison programs, educational opportunities, psychological counseling, and the quality of staff running prisons.

We know that many of the problems of prisons are directly related to overcrowding. Overcrowding contributes to prison violence, and it makes rehabilitation programs and job programs less effective. To relieve overcrowding, we can either build more prisons, which will cost a great deal of money, or reduce the numbers of people in prison. Some states have reduced their prison population by passing laws that allow for only a certain number of inmates to be imprisoned. When that number is surpassed, an emergency is declared—usually by the governor— and certain prisoners are given early release until legal capacity is again reached, when more prisoners must be released. Other jurisdictions have attempted to maintain prisoner population levels by not incarcerating everyone who is arrested.

These solutions present difficulties, for many of these offenders commit additional crimes soon after release or while awaiting trial. However, we know that when more people are placed in facilities the system will cost more money, that the facilities will become more crowded, and that prison administrators will again be faced with the same issues and problems.

The public, our judges, and prison administrators will all have to work together to reach a solution. This solution will include the establishment of a system of checks and balances so that we may continue to protect the public safety, as well as maintain the legal right to punish criminals in a fair and just manner.

We would like to point out that despite considerable debate on this issue, it is said that the United States imprisons more persons than most other countries. According to the former Unitarian Universalist Service Committee's National Moratorium on Prison Construction, "No other country in the world imprisons as great a proportion of the population as does the United States, and the length of sentence for offenders in the American criminal justice system is much greater than that anywhere else in the world."

One way of measuring how a society imprisons its criminals is to compare the number of prisoners in a nation against its population, expressed as the number of individuals for every 100,000 persons. Writing in *The New York Times* recently, the columnist Tom Wicker pointed out that the United States has a prison population of 293 per 100,000. By comparison, South Africa has 333 per 100,000 in prison; the Soviet Union has 268 per 100,000; Australia has 72 per 100,000; and the Netherlands has only 40 persons per 100,000—less than one tenth the rate in America. Part of the reason for the higher rate of imprisonment in the United States is that it has a higher crime rate. This brings us to the question, if prisons are supposed to be so effective, how can we have such a high number of people in prison and such a high crime rate at the same time?

WHAT CAN YOU DO TO PREVENT CRIME?

The most obvious alternative to prison is crime prevention. But crime prevention involves much more than scaring people by threatening punishment for criminal acts.

Young people can take very deliberate steps to be

certain that they do not do anything that is against the law. This is a simple statement, but to put it into action can sometimes be very difficult. Many who become involved in the criminal justice system are not sure how they managed to get themselves into such serious situations. They may have come to crime in small stages—perhaps starting with behavior that did not appear to be a "big deal" at the time.

You will remember, for example, that Cedrick continued to keep his friendships in a group even when he knew that his friends were violating the law. When they allowed him to run small errands, he was flattered. Of course, we all want to be important and accepted.

Sometimes, however, acceptance depends on our "proving" ourselves. This is especially true when there are older kids or young adults involved.

An important part of crime prevention is having the ability to be strong enough not to do what we know is wrong, or even what we think might be wrong, simply because we want to prove ourselves to others. People who are really our friends would never ask us to do anything that would bring us harm. *Are you strong enough to walk away and make new friends, or are you so lonely and so anxious to be included that you would do wrong, just to be part of a group?*

Sometimes young people become bored with their daily routine, especially when they're home alone a lot. Although they have rules about what they should or should not do, their desire for excitement can lead to violations. There's nothing wrong with wanting fun, but plenty wrong with even minor violations. Do you know any people who go in groups or even alone into stores to shoplift? Many young people who shoplift think that it is fun, and they tell themselves that the item stolen is not costly or that the store will hardly miss it. Shoplifting is one of the most frequently committed crimes among young people. You must remember that stealing is against the law and against our moral code.

You will remember that in the beginning of this book we talked about the need for formal laws as well as for certain codes of ethics and behavior, so that people can live together in harmony and with diversity. Unfortunately, some young people belong to families where they have not been taught or where they are not expected to maintain even the most basic codes of behavior. But even these young people know what is legal or illegal, either from what they have learned in school or from watching television.

When the family does not put enough attention on teaching the correct and expected behavior, young people should ask questions and seek information from their teachers, their priests and pastors, their local police officers, and other adult members of the community who are in positions of leadership and respect.

Movies, television, and other media present stories that not only entertain but often fascinate us. Often, characters who are antisocial—who violate the norms of the community—are presented as heroes in these stories. Although the antihero often "wins" in the media, the suggestion that one should be rewarded for criminal behavior should not be taken seriously.

Those persons who prey upon the innocent, who lie, cheat, steal, physically harm, and psychologically persecute others are not to be admired. Do not take them for your heroes. In matters of crime, real life is not much like movies or television. The bad guys most often get caught, if not killed, and they surely do go to jails, prisons, or penitentiaries. Young "bad guys" also get caught, and once they enter the criminal justice system, their lives are seriously altered.

Stereotypical roles for boys often result in young men believing that the test of manhood is to be daring—to take risks with the law. Those who take such risks will often come into direct conflict with the law.

Sometimes children and youth become targets for older youths and adults who want to get them involved in crime. In those instances, *just saying no is not enough.* It is very important that you immediately tell your parent, your teacher, or a responsible adult such as the school nurse or guidance counselor, if someone has asked you to do something that is against the law or against your principles. That person who is trying to involve you needs to know not only that you will say no, but that you have the support and protection of adults.

If you do not know anyone with whom you can talk about such a person, you can *always* talk to the nearest police officer you can find. You can even go to the local police station and tell the officer there that you need to talk to someone about a problem. Seeking the advice of your friends and other young people your age is not the way to solve the problem. *Get adult help.*

It is possible that a very good friend of yours will break the law or begin to associate with people who encourage involvement in criminal activities. You will probably want to try to help your friend. What can you do? Certainly, you can begin by telling your friend that you want to continue the friendship, but that you do not think that your friend's new acquaintances are a good group of people. Try to get your friend to meet other young people or to go with you to participate in a positive activity or hobby.

You should clearly let your friend know that you do not approve of his or her actions and point out the legal consequences that might result. If your friend continues to break the law or to associate with those who are breaking the law, you need to take additional steps. First, tell your parents about the problem. If you do not want your parents to "tell" on your friend, you might talk with any one of the persons mentioned above. They can help your friend. Second, you must realize that you might have to make a decision to give up this friendship, rather than run the risk of getting involved in illegal activities yourself.

In school and among young people, nobody likes a "squealer," and your friend might very well think that you have betrayed him or her if you go to an authority. However, it might be better for you to help keep that person out of trouble than for your friendship to allow the individual to get into trouble. Do all that you can to encourage your friend to talk to someone. If your friend tells you there is no way out of his or her situation, you should immediately discuss the matter *in confidence* with a person in authority. Realize that you might need to say to your friend that you care too much to allow him or her to get into trouble with the law.

When we talked about gangs, we mentioned that many young people become involved in crime through groups that give them a sense of belonging and identity, or something to do. If your family and friends cannot give you the kind of attention or support you need, or if you need something to do with your time, *find an activity:* join an after-school club, volunteer with one of the community programs, or visit the local hobby/craft shop and develop a hobby; talk to a shopkeeper or working person in the community and ask if there is some way that you can volunteer or work.

It is important to remember that very few young people suddenly become criminals. Most often, their involvement in criminal behavior escalates; that is, it becomes more serious over time as they become more daring or confident that they will not get caught. In particular, young people of today are facing a daily barrage of temptations—to get things, to be recognized, to be part of the group, to be "tough," to belong, to impress others. To resist these temptations and crime opportunities means that you walk away *before* you are in a situation where you would break the law or do something that you do not think is right. *Dare* to think for yourself. Be tough-minded and do not allow yourself to be influenced by the crowd. Plan for the future and keep your goals in mind; then you will be less likely to do anything that will upset your course. It is also important to remember that everyone spends periods of time alone. If you like yourself, you do not always need a crowd cheering you into action. The key point here is to like yourself and have a goal that is important to you.

CEDRICK COMES HOME

Once again it is 7:00 A.M. This time, however, it is Cedrick who is waiting to make a journey. Soon an escort guard will be arriving at his room, for Cedrick has been granted parole and will be leaving the prison. He knows that he will now have to behave differently than he did when he was first sent to prison. He anticipates that some of his friends who were not part of the group involved in crime will no longer wish to associate with him. But he also knows that there are some former friends with whom he will no longer associate.

Cedrick learned many things about himself while in prison. Some of those things were hard for him to accept, but accepting them made him stronger and better able to examine those behaviors and attributes that resulted in his imprisonment. He is now a year older, having just celebrated a birthday in prison, which is not something he wants to do again. In the prison, Cedrick met many young men who had problems similar to his. Some of them wanted to change, and some did not. Many had become hardened and embittered by the prison experience.

As Cedrick looks down the long hall that he must walk to get to the room where his parents will be waiting for him, he wonders how they must be feeling. He knows that his father borrowed his uncle's car for this special occasion. Cedrick thinks about how supportive his entire family has been while he was in prison. He promises himself that they will never have to go through anything like this experience again on his account. He will not be coming back, and he will help guide his younger brother and sisters so that they will not make his mistakes.

While in the prison, Cedrick completed his GED (high school requirements for graduation) and he took classes in photography and art. He really liked photography and decided that he would like to continue learning how to be a better photographer. He has already completed papers that will allow him to attend night classes at the local community college; he is interested in taking courses in medical as well as commercial photography.

After being notified that he had been granted parole, Cedrick was assigned to the Needs Assessment Division of the prison, where he and a counselor worked together to design a program that would help him upon his return home. This assistance is sometimes called *mainstreaming*. The counselor gave Cedrick several aptitude tests to determine the kinds of work and study that would be best for him. Then he was assigned to a class to help him improve his math, writing, and speech skills, which will be important when he begins attending the community college.

In prison Cedrick also joined a group of young men who met twice a week to discuss how they would "make it" in their communities and what steps they would take to stay out of trouble. Cedrick felt that this experience had been positive because members of the group had been able to make helpful suggestions to one another.

It was in this group that the young men granted parole learned how often they would have to meet with their parole officer; the importance of maintaining employment; the requirement that they not associate with persons who might be involved in any form of crime; and that they might expect the parole officer to make on-site visits to their homes or places of employment on a regular basis. Cedrick also came to understand that a violation of one of the conditions of parole could result in revocation of parole. He learned that he had lost some of his rights as a citizen;

his state had not taken away his right to vote, but a few states would have. On the other hand, he learned that he could not run for a public office, such as a council member, nor would he ever be able to serve on a jury. Cedrick is probably more fortunate than most of the other young men in the prison because his father arranged for a job interview for him with a company where a friend works. He feels confident about the pending interview because in his speech and communication class he learned how to interview and how to present himself properly. Furthermore, for many years prior to his involvement in crime, he had been a dependable worker at his part-time job. That good work record will be of value to him as he again seeks employment.

Now the guard escorts Cedrick through the final procedures before release. His picture is taken, and he signs the necessary papers and goes through the final checkout point. The new clothes his mother brought him the last time she visited feel strange and stiff after wearing work shirts and jeans for such a long time, but it is good to be able to wear clothing that does not look like everyone else's.

Carrying his bag, and saying his last good-byes, Cedrick stands in the doorway of the waiting room smiling at his mother and father. The door shuts behind him as he hears his father say, "Welcome home, son."

REVIEW QUESTIONS

1. If we didn't have prisons, what do you think we might do with criminals?

2. Do you think the problem of overcrowding in prisons can be solved?
3. Do you think that "Jobs, Not Jails" would keep people from committing crimes?
4. How well do prisons maintain the public safety?
5. Do you think better programs in the prisons would help in the rehabilitation process? How?
6. What would you do if you thought that your friend was involved in criminal behavior?
7. What would you do if a person or persons kept trying to get you to do "errands" or activities for them that are against the law or that you do not want to do?
8. Can you name three people, other than your parents, to whom you can go to discuss problems?
9. When is it a good idea to report someone you know is breaking the law? What is the best way to do this?
10. List three goals that are important to you now. List three goals that you want to achieve as an adult.
11. How can young people find activities that will give them something positive to do with their time?
12. Do you like yourself enough to be alone sometimes?

APPENDIX

RESOURCES

The following organizations are sources of information on prisons and criminal justice. Some offer opportunities for individuals to become directly involved in prison issues such as overcrowding and legislation to provide more money for education, etc.

American Friends Service Committee
1501 Cherry Street
Philadelphia, PA 19102
215-241-7130

National and local criminal justice programs focus on advocacy, education, policy development, and organizing. The national office publishes analysis and action reports. Founded by and related to the Religious Society of Friends (Quakers), but supported and staffed by individuals sharing basic values regardless of religious affiliation. The committee attempts to relieve human suffering and find new approaches to social justice through nonviolence. A corecipient of the Nobel Peace Prize.

CURE (Citizens United for the Rehabilitation of Errants)
c/o Charles Sullivan
11 15th Street NE, Suite 6
Washington, D.C. 20002

Membership includes prisoners and former prisoners, their families, and others concerned with prison reform. Aims to reduce crime through reform of the criminal justice system. Seeks to influence congressional and legislative changes. Write for addresses of state chapters.

Family and Corrections Network
James W. Mustin, Director
P.O. Box 59
Batesville, VA 22924
804-823-6115

Provides information to the public on programs for families involved in correctional systems and assists with program development. Conducts research and publishes quarterly working papers on family programs.

International Association of Residential and Community Alternatives
P.O. Box 1987
La Crosse, WI 54602
608-785-0200

Agencies and individuals working in community-based treatment programs for people who suffer from the image of ex-offender. Purposes are to assist members to function more effectively through the exchange of information on management and treatment, with the goal of helping the socially handicapped achieve a satisfactory return to the community. Also has a program of public information and education in the field of community-based treatment to help communities cope with crime, substance abuse, mental health, delinquency, and related social problems.

NAACP Legal Defense and Educational Fund, Inc.
Contact: Richard Barr
99 Hudson Street, 16th Floor
New York, NY 10013
212-219-1900

Handles cases on general conditions in prison or jail, as well as test cases for inmates. Provides educational and information services.

National Center on Institutions and Alternatives
635 Slaters Lane, Suite G-100
Alexandria, VA 22314
703-684-0373

Serves as clearinghouse and aids in developing and promoting strategies and actions to reduce the number of people involuntarily institutionalized. Develops, promotes, and supervises enduring alternatives to prison programs; attempts to eliminate unnecessary lockup in massive, impersonal prisons and juvenile training schools.

National Convocation of Jail and Prison Ministers
Contact: Rev. Michael Bryant
1357 East Capitol Street SE
Washington, D.C. 20003
202-547-1715

Works toward the abolition of the death penalty; reform of the criminal justice system; and a moratorium on jail and prison construction to encourage the development of alternatives to incarceration.

National Council on Crime and Delinquency
685 Market Street, Suite 620
San Francisco, CA 94105
415-896-6223

An independent, nonprofit organization that develops public policy on criminal justice issues, publishes new theories in the field, sets performance standards, trains volunteers and professionals. Involves citizens in system reform, develops alternatives to traditional methods used by the criminal justice system, and carries on major research projects.

National Criminal Justice Association
444 N. Capitol Street NW, Suite 608
Washington, D.C. 20001
202-347-4900

Members are state and local criminal justice planners, police chiefs, judges, prosecutors, defenders, corrections officials, educators, researchers, and elected officials. Promotes innovation in the criminal justice system through the focused coordination of law enforcement, the courts, corrections, and juvenile justice. Objectives are to focus attention on national issues and developments related to the control of crime; and to determine and effectively express the states' collective views on pending legislative and administrative action encompassing criminal and juvenile justice responsibilities through the development and dissemination of information to and among states.

National Prison Project of the ACLU
Contact: Alvin J. Bronstein
1875 Connecticut Avenue NW, Suite 410
Washington, D.C. 20006
202-234-4830

Part of the American Civil Liberties Union. Handles class action suits involving prison conditions and related issues in state and federal institutions. Litigation is usually limited to cases involving major class actions challenging prison conditions and others of national significance. Also provides advice and materials to other individuals or organizations involved in prison issues. Issues a number of publications as well.

P.E.N. American Center
Prison Writing Program
568 Broadway
New York, NY 10012
212-334-1660

An international organization of poets, essayists, and novelists. Its primary function is to encourage prisoners to use and develop their writing skills. Also provides advice on writing and publishing, and sponsors writing contests for prisoners. P.E.N. is deeply involved in First Amendment issues and works against the imprisonment of dissident writers in other countries.

Prison Pen Pals
Contact: Lou Torok
Box 1217
Cincinnati, OH 45201
606-441-7409

An all-volunteer organization that links citizens with prisoners through mail. Open to men, women, and teenagers in all types of correctional institutions. Write for a list of names and backgrounds of prisoners to choose a person who is imprisoned as a pen pal.

Prisoner Visitation and Support (PVS)
Contact: Eric Carson
1501 Cherry Street
Philadelphia, PA 19102
215-241-7177

Provides visitation to prisoners at all federal and military prisons in the country. Furnishes support services such as supplying books and study materials and maintaining ties with families. With a national network of visitors, PVS maintains contact with prisoners who are transferred from prison to prison and who are in solitary confinement.

The Sentencing Project
Contact: Malcolm Young
918 F Street NW, Suite 501
Washington, D.C. 20004
202-628-0871

Works with the public defender offices and defense counsel to set up alternative program offices in state or public defender offices. Does not provide direct services to prisoners.

U.S. Department of Justice
Civil Rights Division
Washington, D.C. 20530
202-514-6255

Enforces the Civil Right of Institutionalized Persons Act, which authorized the U.S. attorney general to initiate suit against state or local officials who operate institutions in which a pattern of flagrant or egregious conditions deprive residents of their constitutional rights. Has also been active in prisoners' rights cases.

VISITING A PRISON

The following excerpts are from a visitor's orientation handbook at a prison. The rules and regulations for prison visitors are revised from time to time in keeping with the needs of particular facilities. Most handbooks begin with information about transportation services to and from the prison, as well as directions for driving to the prison from the nearest cities. The complete handbook provides information on the following as well:

- festivals and special events
- correspondence
- visiting regulations
- telephone arrangements
- money
- packages.

Guidelines for Family Participation at Special Events

There are special weekend festivals and events. You will receive communication from the inmate if he has made arrangements for you to attend. Only approved family guests may participate. Each inmate will be allowed to invite a maximum of four (4) *family* guests to the event. Included in the category of family are:

father, mother, brother, sister, uncle, aunt, grand-father, grandmother, niece, nephew, cousin, grand-child, son, daughter, wife, common-law-wife (if service unit records show verification). In-laws are allowed to attend if in the company of any of the aforementioned adults.

NOTE: No packages or money will be received for those inmates attending special events.

If you arrive with anyone other than who has been approved to attend this particular event, he/she will not be permitted into the event. Therefore, it is important to find out exactly what arrangements the inmate you are visiting has made. Special events hours are from 9:30 A.M. to 2:30 P.M. As on all visits, proper I.D. is required.

Visiting Regulations

I. Visits are very helpful and we encourage the family to visit often. However, due to the large number of families involved, we ask you to please follow the regulations listed below.

1. Those individuals on the inmate's approved visiting list will be allowed to visit. All persons wishing to visit must complete and return the form requesting to be added to the approved visiting list. All visitors must have approval prior to visiting.

2. Anyone approved under 18 MUST be accompanied by an approved adult when visiting. Unmarried minors under 18 years of age must have prior written permission from their parent or guardian to visit an inmate who is *not* a relative. The written permission may be mailed to the facility in advance or presented by the accompanying adult at the time of the visit.

Such adult will be responsible for the behavior and conduct of the minor while on facility property and for identification of the minor.

Married persons under 18 are emancipated minors. If they are related to an inmate and are on the approved visitor's list, they do *not* need permission or an adult escort, but proof of age and marriage will be required.

Children of inmates will be allowed to visit with prior written permission, as long as no court order prohibiting such visiting is on file with the facility.

3. Visiting privileges may be canceled or suspended when violations of visiting rules and regulations occur either by inmate or his visitor. Visiting regulations are subject to change without prior notice. If visiting privileges are canceled, the visitor shall be notified of his right to appeal the Superintendent's decision. The appeal shall go to the Commissioner.

4. If you are presently on parole or probation, you need written approval from your parole or probation officer and the Superintendent of the Facility.

5. Visitors will not be permitted to bring food, packages, or large handbags into the visiting rooms. Lockers (one per family) are provided outside the visiting room to enable visitors to store packages and large handbags. Foodstuffs or beverages may be purchased by the visitor from the vending machines located in the visiting area. Visitors must purchase food for inmates. Inmates are not permitted to handle money or use the snack machines. One may also purchase food from an authorized outside vendor. See front door officers for menu.

II. VISITATION TO A CORRECTIONAL FACILITY IS A PRIV-
ILEGE WHICH MAY BE SUSPENDED OR REVOKED FOR
VIOLATING ANY ONE OF THE FOLLOWING PROHIBITED
ACTS:

1. The introduction or attempted introduction of contraband into the facility. Contraband is any one of the following articles or things:

a. Any article, thing, or dangerous drug (including marijuana), the possession of which would constitute an offense under any law applicable to the public.

b. Any article or thing which is readily capable of being used to cause death or serious injury, including but not limited to hand gun, shoulder gun, cartridge, knife, or explosives.

c. Any article or thing that is introduced into a correctional institution under circumstances showing an intent to transfer same to an inmate without the permission of the Superintendent or his designee.

d. Any article or thing that is not specifically authorized to be possessed by an inmate pursuant to the rules of the institution wherein the inmate is housed. Alcohol and money are among the items inmates are not permitted to possess.

2. No article may be passed to or from a visitor and inmate. Papers or other articles to be exchanged between an inmate must first be inspected and approved. An inmate may exchange legal documents with an attorney after they have been inspected for contraband by the visiting room officer.

PLEASE BE REMINDED THAT VIOLATION OF THE ABOVE
RULES CAN LEAD TO SUSPENSION OR REVOCATION OF
YOUR VISITING PRIVILEGES AND MAY LEAD TO PROSECU-
TION.

III. Visitors to a correctional facility will be required to furnish proof of identification. Failure to produce adequate identification will result in the denial of a visit. Prior to visiting, visitors shall sign appropriate visiting forms as required by the facility. These records will be maintained by the facility:

1. Adequate identification shall consist of any of the following:

a. Picture I.D.

b. Signature card (credit card, social security card, employment I.D., welfare card, drug program card, Armed Services I.D., driver's license, motor vehicle registration, or any other similar document with the visitor's signature on it).

c. Birth or baptismal certificates shall not be considered adequate information for an *adult* visitor; however, they may be used as identification for a minor child. Absent any other creditable documentation, an adult approved to visit may vouch for the identification of a minor.

2. All visitors will be required to pass through a metal detector and will be hand-stamped before entering the visiting area. There are penalties for introducing contraband into the facility. ALL VISITORS ARE SUBJECT TO SEARCH; HANDBAGS, BRIEFCASES, OR OTHER CONTAINERS SHALL BE SEARCHED AND NO OPEN PACKS OF GUM, CIGARETTES, MEDICATION, ETC., WILL BE PERMITTED BEYOND THE FRONT GATE OF THE FACILITY.

Each inmate will be permitted a maximum of six visitors at any one time on weekdays and four on weekends or holidays. Visiting hours are from 9:00 A.M. through 3:00 P.M., Wednesday through Monday. On Tuesdays only, visiting is from 4:30 P.M. through

9:00 P.M.; also, on Tuesdays, no packages or money may be left for the inmate.

Nothing can be exchanged or accepted from an inmate in the visiting room. Any exchanges must be made through the package room.

Excessive contact, fondling, indecent or other offensive acts which could offend others will not be allowed in the visiting room areas. Acts of this nature, besides disciplinary action, may result in suspension of further visits by the person involved. At a minimum, inmates may kiss at the beginning and end of a visit. Appropriate attire is expected to be worn by visitors; no short shorts, see-through clothing, or plunging necklines, etc.

There is an area for children to play. They must be watched and it is the visitor's responsibility to control their behavior.

Smoking is permitted in the visiting room. Inmates are not permitted to use tobacco products brought in by visitors. Inmates will not be permitted to carry anything from the visiting room after a visit; therefore, they should bring only enough tobacco products to last through the visit.

Visits with attorneys will be in a designated area to ensure privacy in conversation.

All packages left by visitors or received by mail are subject to search.

Items left in packages by visitors which are not allowed must be picked up by the visitor on the way out. It will be the financial responsibility of the inmate to mail home any items which are not picked up after the visit. Items will not be stored.

No articles of any kind will be taken out of the visiting room by inmates.

Inmates or visitors are not to leave the visiting room for any reason without permission of the visiting room officer first.

Separate lavatory facilities are available for inmates and visitors. They must use separate facilities.

CORRESPONDING WITH INMATES

All correspondence should include name and number of inmate for identification purposes. Correspondence should not contain enclosures of any other letters, contraband, cash, drugs, postage stamps, etc. No packages will be accepted for inmates. If you are presently on parole or probation, you need written approval from your parole or probation officer and the Superintendent of the Facility. An inmate may refuse to correspond with any person. Persons not wishing to receive correspondence from inmates must notify the Superintendent in writing. To correspond with inmates in state, federal, or other correctional facilities if you are incarcerated, it must be authorized by both superintendents or their designee, (i.e., counselors). Correspondence with unrelated persons under 18 years of age requires the prior written approval of the minor's parent or legal guardian.

PRISON LIFE

The following excerpts have been selected from what we believe is a typical prisoner orientation handbook. Such handbooks provide the prisoners with the rules, regulations, and other information that will help them understand what is expected of them while they are imprisoned. The handbooks also contain information about most of the services provided to assist them in the areas of rehabilitation, health, education and training, and preparation for future employment. Such handbooks may vary from institution to institution and from state to state.

Although prisoners are not expected to memorize everything in the handbook, they are expected to become very familiar with the rules and regulations that govern the fundamental routines of the day. In particular, they are expected to know the rules and regulations that govern their conduct.

These excerpts cover only four areas of activity; the handbooks are usually dozens of pages in length. The table of contents from this handbook lists more than fifty categories for which there are strict rules, covering everything from identification cards to prisoner marriages.

Cell Cleanliness and Appearance

Upon moving to a new location, inmates are responsible to report any damage to equipment to the housing unit officer. Failure to do so could result in disciplinary action.

Each inmate will:

A. Be responsible for the clean and orderly arrangement of his living quarters.

B. Make his bed neatly upon rising; leaving it neat whenever leaving his cell.

C. Remove wastepaper and trash from living quarters daily and place same in the provided recepticles.

D. Remove all excess plastic jars, tin cans, and other containers from living quarters with the trash. Accumulation of such is prohibited.

E. Keep all unsealed food containers sealed to protect food from dust, insects, etc.

F. Keep all eating utensils in a clean condition.

G. Have no lines, curtains, cardboard or other materials attached to or placed on fixtures or bars.

H. Confine all pictures, photographs, newspaper clippings, etc. to the cell area outlined by the facility.

I. If any equipment or fixtures are in poor condition or not operating, the officer in charge of the company must be notified immediately. If you try to fix plumbing or electrical fixtures on your own, you will be charged under rules regarding tampering with state property.

General Rules

A. Materials will be attached to the block bulletin board in such a way as not to deface this area upon removal of the materials.

B. A privacy curtain will be allowed to be hung in each cell. This curtain is to be used only when the toilet is being used. The curtain cannot be higher than the neck of the inmate in the sitting position. The curtain must be placed around the toilet, *not* the bars.

C. Boisterous and loud conduct will not be allowed.

D. No inmate shall possess more than two (2) packs of cigarettes upon leaving his cell.

E. Shorts or gym clothing will be permitted in the cells, in the gym and yard, except during family or festive events. They will not be worn anywhere else in the facility.

F. For safety reasons, sneakers will not be worn for

work assignments in industrial, vocational, or maintenance shop areas.

G. The wearing of jewelry other than authorized watches, wedding rings, and religious medals is prohibited.

Yard

A. Musical instruments will not be played near the block side of the yard.

B. The building or formation of fences or partitions in the yard is prohibited.

C. Inmates will not be allowed to sit on, nor loiter near the guard posts in the yards. No loitering will be allowed in the yard toilet areas.

D. Group exercise participation in the yards is limited to up to six (6) inmates. The only exception to this rule would be for organized athletic teams during practice or training.

During these authorized group exercise periods, participants may count out loud in unison the number of repetitions of the particular calesthenics. Running or jogging will only be done off the sidewalks and will also be limited to six participants in the exercise yard. There will be no cadence calling or "chanting."

Mess Hall

A. All hats, caps, hairnets, etc., will be removed upon the entering of the mess hall. (Exceptions to this will be made for religious head covering approved by the department.)

B. No containers of any type, i.e., jars, bags,

bowls, or thermos bottles, etc., will be allowed in the mess hall.

C. Proper clothing will be worn in the mess hall. No robes, shorts, warm-up suits, bare feet, shower thongs, sandals or undershirts that expose under-arms.

D. Entrance and exit from the mess hall shall be as the supervisor directs.

E. No food will be passed at the counter. Each inmate must take his own ration. Food may be passed only at the table.

F. Each inmate must take silverware to the counter, whether or not he intends to use it. This silverware must be deposited in the basket upon leaving the mess hall.

G. There will be no skipping seats in the mess hall. Each seat will be filled with your company at all times while in the mess hall.

H. There will be no leaving of seats in the mess hall for any reason, unless authorized by a correction officer or sergeant.

I. There will be no smoking in the mess hall at any time, during the serving of the meal.

J. Inmates will remain seated upon completion of meals, until the officer-in-charge of your company signals or tells you to leave.

K. The first cup of coffee will be obtained at the serving line. If an inmate wants more coffee, he will signal the sergeant or officer, who will then notify the kitchen worker assigned for this purpose.

L. Breakfast meal is mandatory for those who must go to work or school from the mess hall.

GLOSSARY

Acquittal. When a charge against a person is dismissed by the court because there has been a legal decision that the person is innocent.

Antihero. The principal character in a story who does not fit the usual image or expected behavior of a hero. Often, the antihero behaves in a manner that is the opposite of what the majority of the society would expect.

Appellant. A person who seeks an appeal after losing a case.

Appellate court. The court that hears a case on appeal.

Arrest. When a person is taken into custody by a law official (most often a law officer) in order to make a criminal charge against that person.

Assigned counsel. A lawyer appointed by the court who will be paid by the court to represent a person who does not have the money to pay a lawyer.

Bail. A sum of money or item of value that can be paid to the court if a person who has been arrested and charged with a crime does not want to stay in jail until the time to appear in court. If the person fails to appear in court on the correct date and time, that person is said to have "jumped bail" and the money or the item of value (which might be sold) will be taken by the court. In most instances, the process of returning bail money begins when the accused person returns to the court. The process of bail helps ensure that people will return when they are scheduled to appear in court.

Booking. When a person who has been charged with a crime is officially identified (such as by name, height, and other characteristics) and is photographed and fingerprinted. The process of booking takes place when the person is officially charged with the crime by an officer of the law.

Civil case. A law case that is not criminal but is related to individual rights.

Civil rights. Those rights that are guaranteed to each citizen by the Bill of Rights of the U.S. Constitution. An example would be the right to protest against something with which you do not agree.

Classification. The process by which a new prisoner is evaluated and assigned to what the prison administrators decide is best for him or her.

Community. A group of people who live in a given location and who share interests and experiences. These people usually work together for a basic common good. They agree to rules and regulations that bring order and that govern their obligations to one another. There is also some agreed-upon system for leadership and decision making.

Conviction. When the court (the judge or jury) decides that the person is guilty of the crime as charged.

Correctional officers. Staff persons of the justice system who direct or supervise offenders who are imprisoned.

Criminal. A person who has been found guilty of an illegal act, or violation of the law.

Criminal justice system. The many people and places that are part of the official process for identifying crimes, arresting and charging suspects, bringing suspects to trial, determining the punishment of persons found guilty.

Criminologists. People who study crime and the causes of crime as well as the laws of a society.

Defendant. A person who has been charged with a crime and who is involved in the judicial process, which will determine guilt or innocence.

Defense attorney. A lawyer who protects the legal rights of a person accused of a crime.

Deindividuation. The process of ignoring the humanity of another. To reduce another person through one's thought or behavior to a position where he or she is considered to be "less than human."

Detention center. A place of imprisonment on a temporary basis for children and youths who are in the custody of the judicial system and who are waiting for court decisions.

Deterrence. The prevention of crime.

Education. The process by which information is transmitted formally or informally from one generation to another.

Equal protection under the law. The requirement that all persons going through the criminal justice process receive the same just treatment regardless of their race, gender, religion, or other circumstances, including social and economic situation. This requirement is intended to prevent discrimination based on prejudices against any person.

Felony. A serious crime as defined by the legal system, including murder and armed robbery.

Fine. A sum of money that a person who has been found guilty is required to pay to the court.

Gang. A group in which a person has a long-term

membership and loyalty. Many gangs use identifying symbols and customs. Not all gangs are engaged in criminal behavior.

Guards. Staff persons who supervise offenders who are imprisoned.

Illegal. Against the law.

Incarceration. Being in prison or jail or penitentiary or juvenile facility or any other type of judicial institution as a result of sentencing for criminal behavior.

Indictment. A formal statement by a grand jury that there is reason to believe a person has committed a crime.

Inmate. A person who is imprisoned in a judicial institution.

Interactions. When we relate to others through contact that requires us to acknowledge each other.

Jail. A federal, state, or regional facility for the imprisonment of persons awaiting trial and for those convicted of crimes and serving short sentences.

Judge. A person who has been appointed (or sometimes elected) to preside over a court. That person is responsible for the direction of all the court activities and also is the one who can make final decisions about the law of the various cases.

Jury. A group of people who have been determined qualified to serve in a court to listen to the trial of a case and decide whether the defendant is guilty or not guilty. States have specific requirements that must be met by any person who serves as a member of a jury.

Just deserts. The belief that a person who commits a crime should suffer for it.

Juvenile. A young person, usually less than eighteen

years old. The juvenile age is determined by law by each state.

Juvenile delinquent. A juvenile who has been found to be guilty of violations of the law or a constant problem because of negative behavior and who is in need of supervision as determined by the court.

Laws. Rules and regulations of various degrees of importance that have been established by people through their representatives to determine behavior and process. Violation of these laws results in penalties of various degrees of severity.

Magistrate. A judge in one of the lower courts of the justice system.

Misdemeanor. A minor offense for which the punishment may be the payment of a fine, probation, or a short sentence.

National Moratorium on Prison Construction. A nonprofit organization dedicated to the belief that no more prisons should be built. These people believe that alternatives to imprisonment should be explored for many convicted criminals and that more attention should be placed on how poor living conditions foster criminal action.

Norms. Correct behavior expected by a society or by members of particular groups within the society.

Offender. A person who has committed a crime.

Offense. A violation of the law.

Parole. When a person has been released from imprisonment before the end of the sentence and then is supervised by a parole officer.

Parole board. A group of people who decide whether or not an inmate may be released from imprisonment before the end of the sentence.

Parole officer. The person who is the official supervisor and counselor for persons on parole.

Penitentiary. That institution to which the guilty are sent to do penitence—think about their crimes and resolve to change their ways—while in isolation from the community.

Plea bargaining. The process by which an individual may be allowed or encouraged to plead guilty to a reduced charge, which carries less severe sentencing than the crime with which that individual was originally charged.

Police officer. A person who is trained and then authorized to enforce the law, maintain order, and protect citizens.

Prejudice. A predetermined attitude about a person or place that an individual refuses to alter, even when learning that it is incorrect.

Preliminary hearing. A review by a lower court that determines whether there is enough evidence for the accused to appear before a higher court for trial. It is at this level that the accused may make bail in order to stay out of jail while awaiting trial—if the need for a trial has been determined.

Presumption of innocence. The concept that any person who is accused of a crime is to be considered innocent until it has been proven that he or she is guilty.

Prison. A correctional facility for persons sentenced to imprisonment for one year or longer.

Prisonized. Having become adjusted to prison life. If an inmate becomes too prisonized, it may be impossible for that person to function outside the facility because he or she has become conditioned to a highly regimented life that requires no major decision making.

Probation. When a person is sentenced but not imprisoned and placed in the community under the supervision of a probation officer.

Probation officer. An official staff person in the justice system who is responsible for the monitoring and supervision of persons placed on probation.

Prosecution. When actions have been taken to begin and/or conduct legal proceedings against a person accused of a crime.

Prosecutor. A lawyer who represents the government (state, federal, or local) in its case against an offender.

Public defender. A lawyer paid by the government to represent persons in need of such representation but who are unable to defend themselves or to secure a lawyer.

Recidivism. When a person who has served a sentence is released and then continues to commit crime or engage in criminal behavior.

Reformatory. An institution for imprisonment where it is presumed that criminals will change from bad to good.

Rehabilitation. The process whereby an offender can be taught and assisted in learning to obey the law. Some people believe that rehabilitation cannot take place without punishment, but this idea is changing.

Restitution. Payment that is made by a guilty person to the person or persons he or she harmed. The payment may be a specified sum of money or a job that benefits those who were harmed.

Sanction. The condemnation of an individual.

Sentencing. The process whereby a judge determines the treatment (imprisonment, parole, probation, fine, among others) of the person found to be guilty.

Social control. Various means by which members of a society regulate behavior, such as through laws, through discussions and agreement that result in peer pressure, through customs and tradition, or as a result of beliefs that demand particular kinds of behavior.

Social institutions. A system of organization for specific purposes, including the family, the schools, the justice system, religious organizations, the military, and others.

Socialization. The process whereby individuals learn about right behavior, roles, and procedures from the time of birth to death. This learning begins in the home, where parents teach the children. Teaching also takes place in institutions such as schools, as well as through interaction among people.

Society. All people who have a continuing culture in common and who think of themselves as one united people.

Stereotype. An overgeneralized belief about the behavior, or the characteristics of particular persons or groups. Stereotypes can be positive or negative; however, in the area of race, ethnicity, or gender, they are most often negative.

Substance abuse. The improper use of both legal and illegal mind- or mood-altering substances, including alcohol and various chemicals called drugs.

Theft. The act of stealing or the unlawful taking of that which does not belong to you.

Unequal justice. Said to take place when people who

are guilty of the same crime receive different sentences and there are no "reasonable justifications" for the different sentences.

Uniform Crime Reports. The name given to the official information collected about crime and published by the Federal Bureau of Investigation. These reports have been criticized because the method reporting varies extensively—including not only "crimes reported to or observed by the police" but also "crimes that the police have reason to believe were actually committed."

Victimization. The abuse of a person by another, especially when the abuse is through violations of the law.

Violent crimes. Major crimes against people as defined by the FBI, such as robbery, murder, and serious assault.

Warden. The chief administrator of a correctional facility.

White-collar crime. Crimes committed by individuals or corporations through their work, such as consumer fraud and embezzlement.

Witness. A person who testifies about a situation in keeping with what they believe is true.

Work release. A program that allows a prisoner to attend school or work outside their institution of imprisonment. The person must return to the institution at specific times or in keeping with rules and regulations developed for that purpose.

BIBLIOGRAPHY

Prison is a heavy-duty subject, and most of the books on prison are written for an adult readership. The books described here focus on specific topics within the general subject of prisons.

Anderson, George; Hogan, Eileen; Kane, Joseph; and Rivet, Hilton, editors. *Who Is the Prisoner?* New Orleans: The Institute of Human Relations, Loyola University, 1985.
   This publication is a project of the Jesuit Conference of Prison Personnel. It is a Christian response to issues of the criminal justice system. Chapters include "The Criminal Justice System and the Christian Conscience"; "The Hellish Cycle: An Economic Analysis of Crime and Criminal Justice"; "Black Experience of Criminal Justice"; and "Streets That Lead to Jail."

Darnell, Rodger O.; Else, John F.; and Wright, R. Dean, editors. *Alternatives to Prisons: Issues and Options.* University of Iowa School of Social Work, 1979.
   Divided into two sections, this book discusses alternative approaches to social control in several cultures (the Netherlands, China, the United States), as well as creative alternatives to imprisonment for offenders.

Foucault, Michel. *Discipline and Punishment.* New York: Vintage Books, 1979.
   Translated from French, this book presents a history of attitudes and beliefs about crime, antisocial behavior, and punishment. This is done from the points of view of both criminal justice and philosophy. The book is an extraordinary contribution and was favorably reviewed throughout the world.

Georges-Abeyie, Daniel, editor. *The Criminal Justice System and Blacks.* New York: Clark Boardman, Co., 1984.
A collection of contributions by twenty authors from a range of backgrounds. The book focuses on criminal justice and issues of race, ethnicity, and gender. The articles are grouped into categories such as Blacks and crime; Blacks, law enforcement, and the courts; and Blacks in prison.

Krajick, Deving, and Gettinger, Steve. *Overcrowded Time.* New York: Edna McConnell Clark Foundation, 1982.
A highly readable publication that discusses why prisons are so crowded and what can be done about the problem. Part 1 discusses the situation; part 2 presents possible solutions, and part 3 is a resource guide.

Reiman, Jeffrey. *The Rich Get Richer and the Poor Get Prison.* Third edition. New York: Macmillan, 1990.
Focuses on the impact of racism and elitism on the criminal justice system. Most important, the work gives extensive attention to white-collar crime by comparing "the relative danger to the public of criminal vs. noncriminal harms (such as occupational and environmental hazards)." The author supports the view that "those well-off folks who are guilty of white-collar crimes are treated more gently than those poor ones who are guilty of nonviolent property crimes." He concludes that "it also is still true that better-off offenders are less likely to end up behind bars than poor offenders, even when they have committed the same offense."

Unitarian Universalist Service Committee, National Moratorium on Prison Construction. *What Color Are America's Prisons?* Washington, D.C.: 1984.
An intense and statistically documented study highlighting the nonwhite prison population and pointing out racism in the justice system.

Wright, Jack, and Lewis, Peter W. *Modern Criminal Justice.* New York: McGraw-Hill, 1978.

This text, written from a sociological perspective, provides an overview of the criminal justice system. The authors show how certain acts come to be defined as crimes as well as how a person accused of a crime is processed through the system.

BOOKS USED IN PREPARING THIS TEXT

Blackwell, James. *The Black Community: Diversity and Unity.* Second edition. New York: Harper and Row, 1985.

Cherry, Robert. *Discrimination: Its Economic Impact on Blacks, Women and Jews.* Lexington, Mass.: D. C. Heath, 1989.

Goode, William J. *Principles of Sociology.* New York: McGraw-Hill, 1977.

Gordon, Vivian V. *Black Women, Feminism, Black Liberation, Which Way?* Chicago: Third World Press, 1988.

Kamerman, Sheila B., and Kahn, Alfred J. *Privatization and the Welfare State.* Princeton, N.J.: Princeton University Press, 1989.

Madhubuti, Haki. *Black Men: Obsolete, Single, Dangerous?* Chicago: Third World Press, 1990.

Nettler, Gwynn. *Explaining Crime.* Second edition. New York: McGraw-Hill, 1978.

Perkins, Useni E. *Explosion of Chicago's Black Street Gangs: 1900 to Present.* Chicago: Third World Press, 1987.

Prisoners in 1990 Bureau of Justice Statistics. Office of Justice Programs. U.S. Department of Justice.

Reid, Sue Titus. *Criminal Justice.* Second edition. New York: Macmillan, 1990.

Reiman, Jeffrey. *The Rich Get Richer and the Poor Get Prison: Ideology, Class and Criminal Justice,* Third edition. New York: Macmillan, 1990.

Senna, Joseph J., and Siegel, Larry J. *Introduction to Criminal Justice.* Fifth edition. St. Paul, MN: West Publishing, 1990.

INDEX